The Daily Telegraph

A DISPLAY OF LIGHTS
(9)

The Daily Telegraph

A DISPLAY OF LIGHTS (9)

The Lives and Puzzles of the *Telegraph*'s
Six Greatest Cryptic Crossword Setters

Val Gilbert

MACMILLAN

First published 2008 by Macmillan
an imprint of Pan Macmillan Ltd
Pan Macmillan, 20 New Wharf Road, London N1 9RR
Basingstoke and Oxford
Associated companies throughout the world
www.panmacmillan.com

ISBN 978-0-230-71446-5

1 3 5 7 9 8 6 4 2

A CIP catalogue record for this book is available from
the British Library.

Printed in the UK by CPI Mackays, Chatham ME5 8TD

Contents

Acknowledgements

Just as crossword compilers build on the work of previous crossword compilers, so authors build on the work of others. I have drawn heavily on Douglas Barnard's brilliant (but sadly out of print) *Anatomy of the Crossword* and May Abbott's illuminating introduction to *The Daily Telegraph 50th Anniversary Crossword Book*. Father Charles's pamphlet, *The Grand Master*, was also helpful. I am enormously grateful to Ann Tait for sharing her memories of Douglas Barnard; to Enrica Cash for talking lovingly and at length about her husband, Alan; to Lin Danher for the wealth of information on her husband, Bert; to David Twiston Davies for instantly e-mailing me masses of information about past crossword compilers; to Gavin Fuller at the *Telegraph*'s library for painstakingly sending me all the old *Telegraph* crosswords that I needed; to Malcolm Fare for checking my grammar; to Clyde Fare for wrestling with my computer when it would not behave itself; and to Bruno Vincent of Pan Books for not nagging me. Any errors are, of course, mine.

Introduction

The modern crossword was invented in 1913 by Arthur Wynne – the first puzzle appearing in the *New York World* in December of that year.

Wynne was born in 1871 in Liverpool, a city that will crop up again later. His father was editor of the *Liverpool Courier*, but young Arthur wanted to strike out on his own and so emigrated to the United States in his early twenties. He apparently worked for an onion farmer in Texas before reverting to type (in both senses of the word) and taking the job of society editor on an Ohio newspaper. He then became sports editor on a Pennsylvania newspaper and later music editor and critic of the *Pittsburgh Dispatch* – he apparently played second violin in the Pittsburgh Philharmonic Orchestra.

Should you be wondering why I am detailing the life of the long-dead inventor of the modern crossword, it is because the sort of man that he was – with a plethora of interests – defined the puzzle that he invented. A modern crossword will inform you on a whole range of subjects usually caught under the mundane title of 'general knowledge'. Sport, music, literature, politics, history, geography, science, classics and, latterly, computers – by solving crosswords you pick up an inordinate amount of knowledge, which then improves your ability to solve the puzzles, leading to the acquisition of yet more knowledge, and so on. If Arthur Wynne had been a sports journalist all his life, would the puzzle he invented have been the same? No, definitely not; furthermore, he would probably never have been offered the post of editor of the fun section of the Sunday newspaper *New York World*. So what he was and what he was interested in matter a lot to anyone looking at the development of crosswords.

That said, Wynne's puzzles were nothing like the crosswords we know today. He loved puzzles and, one imagines, was particularly interested in the acrostic, a puzzle that dates from at least Roman times. Wynne updated it and created a diamond-shaped grid of interlocking words, calling his creation a 'word-cross'. (The grid for the first puzzle printed in this book, which was indeed the first puzzle the *Daily Telegraph* ever published, will give you some idea of a Wynne grid.)

The word-cross was popular, but hardly took the world by storm. That happened a decade later when two alumni of Harvard, M. Lincoln Schuster and R. L. Simon, brought out the first ever crossword book – with a first print run of 3,600 copies and a retail price of $1.35 (including an attached pencil). It sold more than a million copies in the first year, laid the foundation of the international publishing house Simon & Schuster and triggered a crossword craze which quickly spread across the Atlantic.

On 30 July 1925 the first daily crossword appeared in the *Daily Telegraph* – and it wasn't too dissimilar to the word-cross created by Arthur Wynne twelve years earlier. (Incidentally, crossword lore has it that the name changed from 'word-cross' to 'crossword' because of a misprint. Whether it be true or not, it is apposite, as nothing can incense a crossword solver more than a crucial misprint! However, in this case the mistake stuck.) And to understand those early puzzles, you have to appreciate what had been entertaining British newspaper readers in the teens and early twenties of the last century. They were the traditional word-square, the acrostic and the conundrum – and some of these were seriously difficult!

The word-square was a two-dimensional display of letters, though the display may not have been in a traditional square. One of the earliest – possibly pre-Christian – is the Abracadabra:

```
A B R A C A D A B R A
 A B R A C A D A B R
  A B R A C A D A B
   A B R A C A D A
    A B R A C A D
     A B R A C A
      A B R A C
       A B R A
        A B R
         A B
          A
```

or alternatively:

```
          A
         B B
        R R R
       A A A A
      C C C C C
     A A A A A A
      D D D D D
       A A A A
        B B B
         R R
          A
```

In ancient times these particular word-squares were thought to have magical properties, as the Persian name for the sun god Mithras was Abracadabra, and the ancients may have believed it beyond the power of mortal man to work out how many ways 'Abracadabra' can be read in such a display. Early twentieth-century man worked out that the diamond gives the word 'Abracadabra' in 252 ways and the triangle gives it in 1,024 ways. And remember, early twentieth-century man did not have a computer to tell him that, so it must have taken time and effort; but then he didn't have the distraction of a computer (with its accompanying games), or television, radio and mobile phones, for that matter.

A variation on the word-square was one using different words. One of the earliest examples was found in Cirencester, Gloucestershire, and is now exhibited there at the Corinium Museum. It is a palindromic word-square on a fragment of Roman plaster and it is arranged thus:

```
R O T A S
O P E R A
T E N E T
A R E P O
S A T O R
```

This sort of puzzle – though not in Latin – can be found in newspapers today, with a clue leading to each of the words. But there are two astonishing facts about the Cirencester word-square: firstly, it forms a proper sentence, 'Arepo the sower holds the wheels with force'; and secondly, it is entirely palindromic, i.e. it reads not only from left to right and top to bottom but also, uniquely, from right to left and bottom to top – a feat which has never been emulated. This all goes to prove that the designer of this puzzle had even more time on his hands to use his brain (so to speak) than the afore-mentioned early twentieth-century man.

The acrostic (another brick in the building of the modern crossword) also goes back to ancient times. Psalm 119 is the chapter with the most verses, in the book with the most chapters, in the whole of the Bible. It has 176 verses, which divide themselves up naturally into groups of eight. The reason for this lies in the fact that in Hebrew the psalm is an alphabetic acrostic, with eight verses beginning with each of the twenty-two Hebrew consonants.

The Dutch national anthem, written in the mid-sixteenth century, is an acrostic: the first letters of its fifteen stanzas spell WILLEM VAN NASSOV, one of the hereditary titles of the Dutch king at the time.

Edgar Allan Poe also indulged in acrostics:

Elizabeth it is in vain you say
'Love not' – thou sayest it in so sweet a way:
In vain those words from thee or L.E.L.
Zantippe's talents had enforced so well:
Ah! if that language from thy heart arise,
Breathe it less gently forth – and veil thine eyes.
Endymion, recollect, when Luna tried
To cure his love – was cured of all beside –
His follie – pride – and passion – for he died.

All very fine and literary, but still not much for the solver to chew on.

Enter the conundrum, probably the oldest of the crossword's antecedents, as old as the Sphinx, indeed. For reputedly it was the Sphinx who asked the most ancient of riddles: 'Which creature in the morning goes on four feet, at noon on two, and in the evening upon three?'*

---

* The answer to the Sphinx's riddle, of course, is Man, who crawls on all fours as a baby, walks on two feet in his prime and uses a stick when he grows old. Oedipus replied correctly, and lived to tell the tale.

Introduction

Then there are more complex riddles:

My first is in parties and also in sun
My second is in tea but not in bun
My third is in table but not in chair
My fourth is in cuppa, you're almost there
My fifth is in mad, have you found me?
I rise then disappear when it's time for tea. *

All these types of puzzle could be found in the daily newspapers and weekly and monthly magazines of the late nineteenth and early twentieth centuries – and into this thriving puzzledom landed the crossword on 30 July 1925. It was an instant success, and what had started as a 'six-week diversion' to tempt people into buying a newspaper in the summer lasted for more than eighty years and is still going strong.

The *Telegraph*'s crossword success was not lost on other papers. In 1929 the *Manchester Guardian* printed its first puzzle, followed by *The Times* in 1930, the *Financial Times* in 1966 and, naturally, the *Independent* included a cryptic puzzle when it was first printed in 1986.

---

* *My first is in partieS and also in Sun*
   My second is in Tea but not in bun
   My third is in tablE but not in chair
   My fourth is in cuppA, you're almost there
   My fifth is in Mad, have you found me?
   I rise then disappear when it's time for tea. – STEAM

These are now the 'Big Five' in the world of British cryptic crosswords – yes, there are others and there are more difficult puzzles that crop up in the Sunday papers and magazines, but for the dedicated cruciverbalist (a word that first appeared in the early 1980s, meaning a person who compiles or solves crosswords) the 'Big Five' are the ones that punch above their weight six days a week. And the cruciverbalist followers of each paper will swear that their puzzle is harder, fairer, wittier, etc. than that of any of the other newspapers. Now you might think that the readers of national newspapers choose their paper on the basis of political leaning, columnists or news coverage, but research shows that the crossword plays a big role in an individual's choice.

So what makes the *Telegraph* crossword unique to the *Telegraph* and the *Guardian* crossword unique to the *Guardian*, and so on? As I was crossword editor for the *Daily Telegraph* for thirty years, I would love to say that it is the steadying hand of a newspaper's crossword editor that makes the difference. But I would be lying. What the crossword editor does is titivate the icing on the cake, making sure it's elegant and enticing, but if the cake underneath has been badly made the icing will fool nobody. In the matter of crosswords, it is the compilers who are the bakers of the confection, and they who make or break the crosswords.

Each of the Big Five has a team of crossword compilers; some will create puzzles for only one newspaper, whereas others will work for all five.

The *Telegraph* has been fortunate in all its compilers. But it has had the benefit of six outstanding puzzle creators, from L. S. Dawe, who was the first man to accept the challenge of creating a daily crossword for a British newspaper (truly *terra incognita*) and who compiled only for the *Daily Telegraph*, to Roger Squires, who has compiled for all the Big Five, was in the *Guinness Book of Records* as the most prolific crossword compiler and is still contributing his elegant and faultless puzzles to *Telegraph* readers on a Monday.

Running in tandem with Dawe for a few years before taking over the senior compiler baton was Douglas St P. Barnard, whose elegant puzzles set a standard only matched by his colleague Alan Cash. They were joined in the late 1970s by Bert Danher, who could do more things with anagrams than any single man had a right to. In the 1980s, as Barnard and Cash entered their last years, Ruth Crisp entered the fray with clues that were so sharp and elegant they could cut you.

To any solver of the *Daily Telegraph* crossword these six compilers – Dawe, Barnard, Cash, Danher, Crisp and Squires – should have their names blazing out on high in lights. And indeed they do, for one of the meanings of the word 'light' is 'clue'. And these six compilers were, in both senses of the word, the leading lights of the *Telegraph* crossword.

This book features a dozen puzzles from each of these six compilers, spanning in total more than eighty years. Each compiler has a preface devoted to them, their style, their life and the events that were going on around them, from the General Strike, Great Depression and the Second World War while Dawe was creating puzzles, to the millennium bug scare and the Twin Towers tragedy of the present day, when Roger Squires's crosswords were printed.

But I have still to mention the last piece in the crossword jigsaw – you the solver, without whom everything is for naught. I reckon there are millions of crossword solvers in Britain, and a good few hundred thousand of them tackle the *Telegraph* crossword. When the *Telegraph* published its eightieth birthday crossword on 30 July 2005, the puzzle contained clues from all the compilers that the newspaper had employed over those eighty years (tricky, but, thanks to the wonders of modern technology, possible). We also ran a clue competition for solvers, and the winning three entrants had their clues included in the birthday puzzle.

Ian Glegg was one of those three winners, and it is his clue that forms the title to this book, *A Display of Lights (9)*. The solution was, of course, 'crossword', a crossword being an array of clues (lights). But it also seemed a fitting description of the six *Telegraph* compilers whose work is featured in this book – *A Display of Lights (9)*, solution: 'compilers'.

VAL GILBERT
Telegraph crossword editor 1976–2006
30 July 2008

Leonard Sidney Dawe

The astonishing crossword-compiling career of Leonard Sidney Dawe, spanning almost forty years, has been hijacked by his part in the *Telegraph*'s D-Day crossword *cause célèbre*, when several D-Day code words appeared as solutions in the *Telegraph*'s cryptic crosswords in the two months prior to D-Day. But that occurred some twenty years into his compiling career, which had started in the most extraordinary way.

The first *Daily Telegraph* crossword appeared on 30 July 1925 and nothing quite like it had ever been seen before in a daily national newspaper. Acrostics, conundrums and word-squares were familiar to most newspaper readers, but a crossword was something entirely new and, according to some, new-fangled. Therefore it was not surprising that the paper's acrostic expert, having been sounded out about taking on the crossword, retorted that he 'wouldn't touch it with a bargepole'.

Quite how Leonard Dawe got to be offered the job is lost in the mists of time, but one does get the distinct feeling that it must have been by word of mouth. How else would a senior science master at St Paul's School, London, end up compiling a new type of puzzle for a national newspaper?

We know very little of Dawe's early life, but he was born around 1890 and therefore it seems likely that he served during the First World War and then took up a teaching career on his return to Civvy Street. His photograph portrays an austere-looking individual, but this is not borne out by his writing or his crossword puzzles, which could be quite frivolous, with, on occasion, words made up to fit the grid.

In 1961 he wrote an article in the *Daily Telegraph* on how to compile crosswords, opening with the words: 'It might be supposed that, having compiled more than 5,000 *Daily Telegraph* crossword puzzles, it would be easy to show the uninitiated just how it is done.' More than 5,000 puzzles? That's around three puzzles a week for thirty-six years! In 2001 the *Telegraph* printed an article celebrating the thousandth *Daily Telegraph* crossword by Ruth Crisp (another compiler celebrated in this book). She was a mere novice compared to Dawe. He went on to advise would-be compilers to use a pencil (lightly!) and to be prepared for 'the use of india-rubber and fresh ideas'. He concluded: 'The only really competent teacher of this subject is experience, to which the fumbling author of that ghastly first *Daily Telegraph* crossword puzzle . . . now acknowledges his great indebtedness.'

And he was right on both counts – only experience makes a good crossword compiler and that first crossword really was awful! It is included in this book as a curiosity, so do not try and solve it – you will only find the experience depressing.

In fact, most of Dawe's puzzles will be extremely difficult for the modern solver, but it is fascinating to see how his puzzles developed over four decades of the twentieth century. In that first puzzle the clues are entirely dependent on general knowledge, but the modern solver would even quibble about that. For example: 45 Across 'First name of famous American author' – 'Well, could we whittle it down a little bit?' the modern solver would complain, and the same waspish response would be evoked by several of those clues. But, as the introduction to this book outlined, solvers in those days were used to riddles and conundrums, so would find such clues quite acceptable. And as to the pattern, does not its centre look exactly like that Abracadabra diamond? Again, very familiar to the 1920s solver. Such wide chunks of white made life much easier for the solver and ridiculously difficult for the compiler. No wonder Dawe wrote: 'To begin with choose a pattern . . . with a minimum of wide open spaces.'

Another thing that will perplex the modern solver is the lack of information about the make-up of the solution words – the number(s) in brackets after the clue showing how many letters are in the solution was not part of the crossword until 1936. So in that first crossword the solver would have no idea that 8 Across was hyphenated (1-4), they had to just work it out for themselves – riddles and conundrums again.

Dawe was certainly innovative. On 8 November 1927 (the second crossword in this book) his offering was a thematic crossword – on doctors and dentists. It is also an instance of where he found himself, in his own words, 'heading for trouble'. Twenty-nine Across 'This has its tail dislocated' has the solution 'Sthi', which, you will not be surprised to learn, is not a word. It is the letters formed from the solutions around it 'in a wide open space'. I suspect that Dawe just didn't have the heart to start all over again, so settled for an anagram of 'This' with its tail dislocated, i.e. the 's' at the end moved to the front. *Nul points*, Mr Dawe! But no doubt the solvers of the day just shrugged their shoulders and moved on . . . A year later he produced the clue 'Change a battle to a range', which is both cryptic clue and riddle. The cryptic element is in the word 'range', which in the context of the clue seems to be about the range of a weapon; but in fact refers to a mountain range. And the riddle element? The 'battle' is the Battle of Sedan (Franco-Prussian War, 1870) and an anagram of Sedan is 'Andes' – the range in question and the solution to the clue. Just run of the mill to the 1920s crossword solver, but exceedingly difficult to his or her modern counterpart, particularly as we have now moved to the modern pattern with no wide open spaces! Dawe was learning his trade very quickly.[*]

---

[*] There is no way after the passage of more than eighty years to categorically prove that these twelve puzzles were created by Dawe. His fellow compiler Melville Jones, another master at St Paul's, also

During Dawe's compiling career the changing nature of the crossword matched the changing nature of the world. On the big stage of national and international affairs the 1920s saw momentous events. In early 1925 the serum run to Nome, or the 'Great Race of Mercy', relayed diphtheria antitoxin by dog sledge across Alaska to combat an epidemic, a race still re-enacted to this day. In 1926 the General Strike was called, in 1928 parliament passed the Women's Suffrage Bill and in 1929 the New York Stock Exchange collapsed triggering the Great Depression. But life continued serenely in some quarters. On 30 July 1929 the *Daily Telegraph* reported of the Eton College Regatta: 'Although not on so large a scale as last year, the racing provided considerable amusement and excitement for a large number of spectators. Mr W. D. C. Erskine Crum, the second captain of the boats, officiated as starter and judge.' Starter and judge? Tut, tut – wouldn't be allowed nowadays!

The 1930s saw the rise of Nazism and the outbreak of the Second World War but there were other aspects to the decade. The 'bodyline' Ashes Test series took place, radar was invented, the first frozen foods were sold, the BBC started a regular television service and both the Empire State Building and Sydney Harbour bridge opened. And the *Daily Telegraph* published its first crossword book – price 2s 6d (12½p in decimal currency). The newspaper still had time for the human

---

compiled three a week, but I am confident that these dozen puzzles *are* Dawe's because of the style and content. Trust me!

interest story, or, in this case, the animal interest, when in July 1932 the *Daily Telegraph* published a picture with the caption 'Billy, a baby hippopotamus from Portuguese Angola who will be on public view at the London Zoo today for the first time since his arrival in this country'.

In 1936, as mentioned earlier, numbers in brackets started appearing after *Daily Telegraph* clues, alerting solvers to the number of letters in the solution word(s). This went hand in hand with the crossword pattern emerging in the format that we know it today and the inclusion of more cryptic clues:

Clue: A two-face humorist? (5)
Solution: *Twain*

Clue: Fruitful appeal to maintain existing
state (5)
Solution: *Olive*

Clue: As sheltered as the contents of a book
(two words – 5,5)
Solution: *Under cover*

This sort of clue was becoming increasingly prevalent in the 1930s. But the crosswords of the late 1930s had an increasing number of military and war references. War was in the air.

The D-Day *Telegraph* crossword affair has been covered in detail in another *Telegraph* crossword book so I will not cover it again here.* But I have included

_____

* *The Daily Telegraph: 80 Years of Cryptic Crosswords* by Val Gilbert.

three of the D-Day puzzles in this book, each one containing a D-Day code word: the Dawe puzzle of 22 May 1944 contained the solution word 'Omaha'; on 30 May 1944 'Mulberry' appeared; and on 1 June 1944 one solution was 'Neptune'. Deliberate or coincidental? The argument still rumbles on . . .

What is not so well known is the prequel to the D-Day crossword affair, and that was the Dieppe débâcle – which was, in some ways, more serious. Two days before the disastrous Dieppe raid in August 1942 the clue 'French port' (6) appeared in the *Daily Telegraph* crossword (the seventh puzzle in this book). The next day, 18 August, the solution, 'Dieppe', was printed; and on 19 August the raid on Dieppe took place. The objective had been to seize and hold a major port for a short period, both to prove it was possible and to gather intelligence from prisoners, as well as rounding up captured materials, while assessing the German responses. No major objectives of the raid were accomplished: 3,623 of the 6,086 men who made it ashore were either killed, wounded or captured. The Allied air forces failed to lure the Luftwaffe into open battle, and lost 119 planes, while the Royal Navy suffered 555 casualties.

As Roger Squires (a compiler also featured in this book) has written: 'The possibility of passing intelligence by crosswords may sound far-fetched, but they were used for secret communication by anti-Nazis in 1934 and banned in liberated Paris to avoid similar use.' The War Office certainly did not think it far-fetched, and Lord Tweedsmuir (the son of the novelist John

Buchan of *The Thirty-Nine Steps* fame) was called upon to investigate the crossword. Tweedsmuir was at that time a senior intelligence officer attached to the Canadian Army, which made up the main assault force for the Dieppe venture. Later he commented: 'We noticed that the crossword contained the word Dieppe, and there was an immediate and exhaustive inquiry which also involved MI5. But in the end it was concluded that it was just a remarkable coincidence – a complete fluke.'

Fluke or not, the puzzle had been compiled by 'Moneybags', as Dawe was known to the pupils of Strand Grammar School, where he was now head-master. Leonard Sidney Dawe, L. S. Dawe, L. S. D. (pounds, shillings and pence in the old money), hence 'Moneybags' – his pupils had obviously caught the cryptic crossword bug!

Dawe rode out the crossword scandals of the war years and continued to compile into the 1950s against the backdrop of the Festival of Britain, the Korean War, the Suez crisis, the start of nuclear bomb tests, the death of George VI and the coronation of Elizabeth II. But the *Telegraph* also reported the lesser events: on Tuesday 5 March 1957 a paragraph on the back page stated:

Mr Herbert Hoover, the former President, who is 82, announced on television last night that he is writing a book about one of his favourite figures, Woodrow Wilson. He said all Presidents and many Prime Ministers become anglers and he concluded that this was because fishing and prayer were the only activities in which they could obtain a little privacy.

All very fine in 1957, but you could be forgiven for thinking that in the twenty-first century, after Bush and Blair, the private activities of leaders have been reduced to one – fishing!

To go back to the 1950s, when in 1958 the *Daily Telegraph* printed its ten thousandth crossword, guess who compiled it? Yup, you're right – it was Dawe, and for this special occasion he burst into verse. Not very good verse, but verse nevertheless, as you will see in the twelfth crossword in this book.

Dawe was now in his late sixties and his compiling days were nearly over – he died in 1963, still in harness. In modern terms, his cryptic crosswords were not of the highest quality: he still had a fondness for the word 'This' when referring to a solution, which was a hangover from the days of riddles and conundrums. However, he is a colossus in the world of British crosswords, the trailblazer who went on to shape the crossword in all its facets – the clues, the patterns and the solutions – into the puzzle that we know today. The current format of the crossword was created by Dawe: since his death very little has changed, and were his ghost to pick up a *Daily Telegraph* crossword today, he would probably be able to solve it . . .

1

30 July 1925: First crossword printed in the *Daily Telegraph*

ACROSS

1 Author of *Childe Harold*
5 Author of tales of mystery
8 Will reveal the hidden
13 Incursion
14 Elizabethan sea-rover
16 Lily
17 Succulent plant
18 Useful in haymaking
19 Nap
20 Where cricketers are trained
21 A distinguished order
22 Adverb
23 Chinese coin or weight
25 A seaside pleasure
28 Cut
30 Soothing; product of Gilead
34 A blemish except in a billiard ball
35 Shakespearian character
37 A word from the motto of the Garter
39 A seaside implement
40 Where Sir John Moore died
41 Travellers' haven
42 Selvage
44 Part of a ship
45 First name of famous American author
46 Unadulterated
47 Petition
48 Beverage
53 King of the Amalekites, who came 'delicately'
57 Military abbreviation
59 That is
60 A measure
63 Cromwell's 'Empty bauble'
64 Island home of an ancient civilization
66 The germ of a building
67 A volcano
68 Guarded by eunuchs
69 Kind
70 Visionaries
71 Applied to anything perfect
72 A people with unalterable laws

DOWN

1 Often 'snatched from the burning'
2 A seat of learning is the key to this
3 Tumult
4 Poems
5 Bears the burden of youth
6 Tree
7 Supplements
9 Transported
10 Air (mus.)
11 An annual festival
12 A fish
14 Fall
15 Greek god of love
24 Mythical founder of a great Empire
25 Country of Europe
26 Not so well
27 Pronoun
28 Indian lemur
29 A district in South London

31 Conjunction
32 River of France
33 Can pick and strike
34 Note of octave
35 First name of famous
   Highland outlaw
36 Unit
38 An explosive
43 Thank you
45 Exist
49 A king, both first and sixth
50 A German word not used
   on Armistice night

51 Consider
52 Depressions
54 Bars and is often barred
55 A skin affliction
56 Changed by motorists
58 Rock
59 Also
60 Recess in a church
61 Lump
62 Would apply to the
   upper atmosphere
65 Before

2

ACROSS

1 We owe much to these men – but they prefer to be paid
4 When we put these out it is for the doctor's benefit
8 Best of all medicines
10 Doctors can do nothing to this youth
12 This lies in consulting the doctor at your peril
13 What prescriptions are in
15 Extracted from us by dentists
16 Abbreviated 8 Across
17 If you don't this any better for the treatment, tell him so
19 Medical opinions do not always this
21 In a perfect world doctors would be this
22 Time when the patient hopes to be well again
24 The successful consultant's patients are this
26 The dipsomaniac's trouble
27 Many diseases are traceable to a little this
29 This has its tail dislocated
31 A medical this often puzzles the patient
34 This is heard by 40 Across
35 Lymph used in vaccination in this
38 The gouty patient's trouble
39 Don't offer this in payment to 28 Down
40 Doctors apply the stethoscope to these
42 Also to this

44 Sick-room slang in connection with fever
45 Dentists' livelihood
46 Being this for himself is the hypochondriac's trouble
47 We should prefer these surgical instruments to have an additional S
48 Often used in cases of poisoning

DOWN

1 Artificer in gold and ivory
2 Sufferers from gigantism are this
3 If the patient tries to walk too soon he may this
5 This wound needs antiseptic treatment
6 This powder is given to infants
7 If your doctor is not this, you may be all but the first letter
8 Articles of fruitarian diet
9 Cause of 15 Across
10 Doctors recommend this fruit
11 This youth is apt to need medical attention
14 The dyspeptic should avoid this
18 *Mens sana in corpore sano* is a good one
19 Symptom of tarantulism
20 Sufferer in the dentist's chair does this to 15 Across
21 When your liver is this you feel rotten
23 Exclamation often heard by the dentist

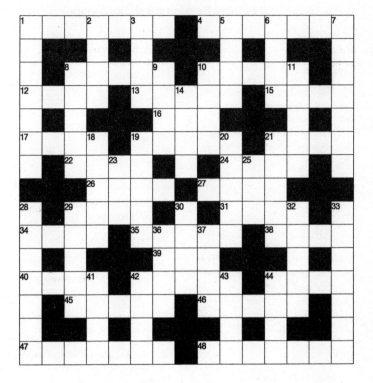

25 If you this nine pork chops, you were asking for it

28 M. Poincaré's medical adviser

29 Primitive medical appliance used by Job

30 Drug

32 You should not withhold this from your doctor

33 Surgical instruments should be this

36 This complexion is a bad sign

37 Don't this too much about your health

41 If you do this for the doctor, you should take his advice

42 This is what you are to the doctor

43 A famous doctor went on a this in the Hebrides

44 Mr Gladstone cut this down in order to keep fit

3

6 November 1928: Herbert Clark Hoover wins
US presidential election

ACROSS

1 This and monopoly do not agree
8 Not a polite bandit
10 'Where the sacred river ran' (Coleridge)
12 Things do not go smoothly for this OT character
14 Change a battle to a range
17 Deck
19 Pluralize, and find edibles
20 The track for this contest requires no preparation (two words)
21 Pinch and pull
22 Hidden in 'You think, Edward, that justice is lame in Fermoy?'
23 A shaper of scenery
24 Town in Surrey
25 Often a colour out of place
26 Even a blind man can spot this animal on occasion
29 Gregarious animals are seen in this
31 Kind of gull
32 Hardly graceful
33 Not infrequently visit 10 Downing Street

DOWN

2 Indian province
3 For this Eastern the fires of the heart are evidently burnt out
4 A suit of this should have a small waist
5 Luggage, perhaps
6 Musical instrument
7 Applicable to what happened recently at Charfield
9 Basic
11 Charles I had no reason to dub his successor this
13 For dinner conversations
15 English county
16 Excusable if you are successful in 1 Across
18 This people wear nothing but skins
19 Parts of leaves, or bodies
26 View

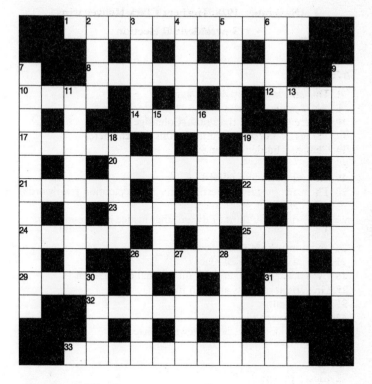

27 A learned Eastern
28 A war-time habit
30 Coin
31 Bemuse

4

27 December 1932: Radio City Music Hall opens
in New York

ACROSS

1 Inlying contrast in exceptional form
8 Turkey's ally in promoting internal disorder
11 Might have been wary, but is not straight
12 Part of a meringue
13 There's quite a notion in this military weapon
15 S. American republic
16 More than twelve months – long, isn't it?
17 Playful allusion to a partridge, perhaps
18 This deity is mostly the 'big noise'
19 Father has an interest in this foreign fruit
21 Starting again with something fresh in foreign currency
22 'Same rig' (anag.)
23 This may come in useful when nurse dresses you
26 This is what part of NB stands for
27 One has a brush with this at night
28 A soldier

DOWN

2 It isn't fair!
3 A much-reduced account
4 Chemical brought to bay in the I. of W.
5 Nude dog causes resentment
6 Nothing on in a certain direction
7 This dainty sounds as if it observed the professor taking a turn or two
8 In the ascendant
9 The architect of the golfer's last hole
10 Still bright
14 The lion is merely a variation of this
15 Fish are mixed inside
19 Artist whose head is one big ache
20 A surviving partner
24 Make a book from a speck
25 About the last thing some Americans are put on
26 Abet in other way to form a foreign letter

Leonard Sidney Dawe

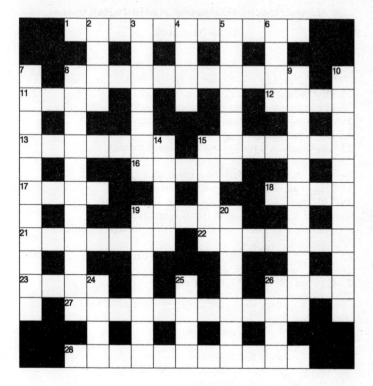

5

20 August 1936: Start of Stalin's Great Purges in Moscow

ACROSS

1 One of the things a domestic should manage to grasp (10)
8 A small part of the Ontario tableland (4)
10 A complimentary emotion, and you may see the confused lass with her share (10)
11 Tree that may be long (4)
12 Put here anything you do not want (4)
15 This puts off the evil day (7)
18 The unscrupulous may think this pays, but it is mostly a frost (5)
19 This often finds itself in the soup (5)
20 Rather hazy suggestion of a few with the shivers (5)
21 A tuneful Scot (5)
22 This is the limit (5)
23 This valve is part of a motor engine (5)
24 A two-faced humorist? (5)
25 This river is nearly filled with useless vegetation (5)
26 This is as hard as the ingrate can become (7)
30 A nautical tuck-in (4)
33 This suit is not for the old (4)
34 Come again (10)
35 Drag in robust fashion (4)
36 This brings down the house, of course (10)

DOWN

2 In this a hack might put one off (4)
3 Fruitful appeal to maintain existing state (5)
4 This bad lad has swallowed a bit of machinery (5)
5 I do it in another way (5)
6 The benevolent sort (4)
7 Check like part of a plant (4)
9 If his gambles go wrong he sometimes loses his head and becomes a criminal (10)
10 Destroy (10)
13 The dear nun has not achieved a superior situation (10)
14 The art of the actor lies in this (10)

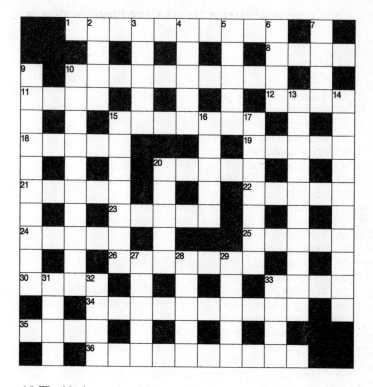

15 The ideal town in which to while away the idle hour (7)
16 A bar (5)
17 Lift (7)
20 One abode is like half-a-dozen all topsy-turvy (5)
27 An actual number is the making of the kingdom (5)
28 The home of the Gurkha (5)
29 Fish (5)
31 Early OT character (4)
32 A male name in short (4)
33 This should help a Dutchman to speak double Dutch (4)

6

ACROSS

5 Nearly most of it is final (6)
8 The summons of war (three words – 4,2,4)
9 Fat overlapping of adjective of altitude (6)
10 As sheltered as the contents of a book (two words – 5,5)
11 This kingdom contains no trees (6)
12 This action would set the village on fire (10)
17 This ends curiously (3)
18 A captain may leave it with his mate (5)
20 Episode in the story of a sweep (4)
22 To a high degree (4)
23 River mostly torn (5)
24 Time for a gunner (3)
26 There is this in 23 Across and yet there probably is not!
   (two words – 5,5)
30 One finds these low in the country (6)
31 Quite allowable but the second I can go and leave a friendly
   warning to retreat (10)
32 Unhappy husbands are often kept at it, they say (6)
33 Harmonious (10)
34 Mostly, and altogether, not heavy (6)

DOWN

1 A loud-mouthed upholder of the doctrine of force (6)
2 One of the things that comes straight from the shoulder (6)
3 Obliged, and given food when the sea creature has gone (6)
4 Much the same as 34 Across (7)
5 Off the route (6)
6 Commonly known to figure at school when least common (8)
7 How will he fare for fare without fare (8)
13 Hearty alternative: choice of letters (4)
14 Mostly a fresh little creature (4)
15 Translate the last two letters into English and more people
   could live on it (5)
16 This water is in the North of England (5)

18 Swear (4)
19 Gait (4)
20 Read part of it certainly but you will find it shocking (8)
21 Put whatever you wish here (8)
25 Kind of voice in which the bridegroom should say 'I will' (7)
26 Take your pick (6)
27 The doctor may advise it, but no toil may produce it (6)
28 Britain didn't have to give a girl a weapon to defeat it (6)
29 Range (6)

7

17 August 1942: US raid on the Japanese-occupied island of Makin

ACROSS

1 This is weighty when without its head (6)
4 Complaisant though exercising compulsion (8)
9 A foreign stamp (6)
10 A song about the USA for a drinking bout (8)
12 Length of poetic work (5)
13 The quantity required to make a great egg (9)
15 Used to be shaped by the pen-knife (3)
16 Fish (5)
17 The kind of sieve that presents some difficulty (6)
22 An establishment where the charges are small (6)
24 A steep ascent but not as bad as it seems (5)
27 Dance step (3)
28 Butterfly that a fruiterer might give a child for running an errand (two words – 6,3)
31 Social scale (5)
32 Ornamentation that keeps a boat on a level keel (8)
33 Primitive boat (6)
34 Naturally a correct weapon (two words – 5,3)
35 Epithet for the arguments about fuel rationing (6)

DOWN

1 I'm in part of the States to find the value (8)
2 Common commonsense (8)
3 Agony, or makes a bit of a teaser (9)
5 Oriental narcotic (5)
6 I have nobody beside me when I hole thus (two words – 2,3)
7 Put to the yoke (6)
8 Old vessel now only part of a modern one (6)
11 Material (6)
14 Part of 17 Across which we want to get in wars (3)
18 French port (6)
19 Dish that may be cooked in 8 Down (9)
20 Curtailed yet is there (two words – 3,5)
21 Influenced but artificial (8)

Leonard Sidney Dawe

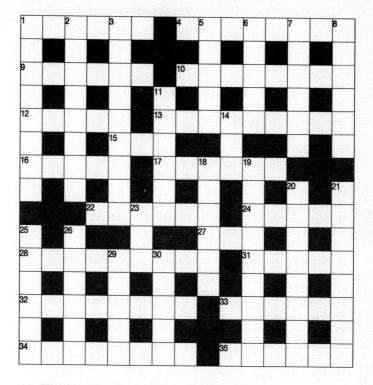

23 'The fairest of her daughters ——' wrote Milton
paradoxically (3)

25 The worker for a drink (6)

26 When television in colour comes in this fault will be
doubly one (6)

29 Musical scale (5)

30 General purport (5)

8

22 May 1944: D-Day code word 'Omaha' appears in the *Daily Telegraph* crossword

ACROSS

1 A shot that falls short is not thus satisfactory
(four words – 2,2,3,4)
9 Town of Germany (5)
10 'Call Ina home' (anag.) (11)
11 The Derby winner to start a branch of mathematics (5)
12 Tree used in the building of the Temple (5)
15 Town to go down in times of drought (5)
17 Drink upset in 10 Across (3)
18 To get this fabulous lady just ponder (4)
19 Ecclesiastical assembly (5)
22 Its sole work is to produce some effect (5)
23 Not obsolete (two words – 2,3)
24 Battle of the last Great War (5)
26 One probably this these represented at a 19 Across (4)
27 The start of 35 Across (it's given you) (3)
28 This worker is as good as five in the RN (5)
30 The way in which a tasty lemon might come in useful (5)
33 An overworked word nowadays for 'rate' (5)
35 This gives vagueness to place or number (11)
36 Lightweight of the animal world (5)
37 The credit for a joint thus perfectly cooked should go to
the turnspit (four words – 4,2,1,4)

DOWN

2 This meal would be nit by bit (5)
3 Red Indian on the Missouri (5)
4 Wine (4)
5 No small deer (5)
6 He wrote 'A thing of beauty is a joy for ever' (5)
7 By sticking to one's work (11)
8 A mere jumble of words (11)
12 At any rate a writer of music should have this to offer
importunate creditors (11)
13 Kind of absentmindedness (11)

Leonard Sidney Dawe

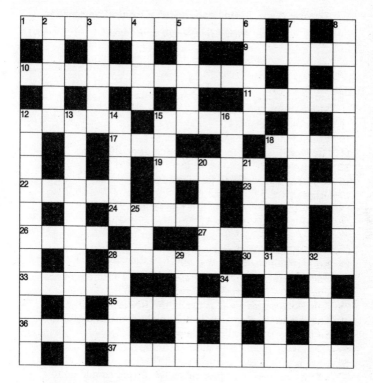

14 Gathering in which all take part (5)
15 This continental river might easily become a drain (5)
16 Sign of the Zodiac (3)
20 Displeasing (5)
21 One of the worldly wealthy (5)
25 Stands for the control of the Thames (3)
28 Well-known refusal given to the lad (5)
29 Edge (5)
31 Fish that resists your getting him his tail (5)
32 Afterwards (5)
34 This term for European of sorts seems to be 500 years old (4)

9

30 May 1944: Princess Charlotte Grimaldi resigns
her right to the throne of Monaco in favour of her son,
Prince Rainier

ACROSS

1 'Wandering near her secret bower molest her ancient ——
reign' (Gray) (8)
5 Danger courted by billiard players (6)
9 His weapon is the pen (8)
10 Tenant of a kind (6)
11 This bush is a centre of nursery revolutions (8)
12 It is no use asking a jazz band to play for this dance (6)
14 An early example of the NAAFI girl? (10)
18 The stronger his team the less this member of it has to do (10)
22 The dim distance (6)
23 'Eager set' (anag.) (8)
24 The words that stick in the mouth of the suffragette who has
found a husband? (two words – 2,4)
25 Courteous though exercising compulsion (8)
26 Epithet for that story of the ivy that strangled a sleeper (6)
27 An old week (8)

DOWN

1 A suitable opening word (6)
2 Not so long ago (6)
3 This great English painter does not sound like any Cubist (6)
4 If there are grounds in the coffee the cook should be this
and the coffee this before serving it (10)
6 Did a nose get out of order? This may be the cause (8)
7 Of various kinds as arranged (8)
8 Man's justice (8)
13 We this men's deaths; it's very sad (10)
15 'Coasting' (anag.) (8)
16 Not the same as a liking for veal (two words – 4,4)
17 Only on the surface (two words – 4,4)
19 Gracious (6)
20 The kind of fence to lose colour (6)
21 The motive force for a grandfather clock (6)

Leonard Sidney Dawe

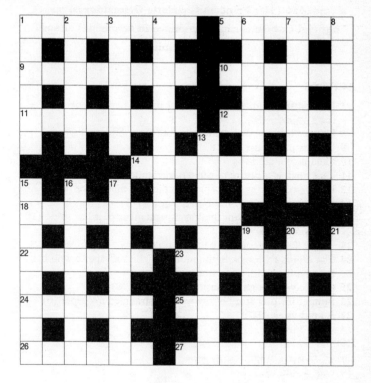

10

1 June 1944: BBC transmits coded message to resistance fighters in France warning that the invasion of Europe is imminent

ACROSS

1 'Lid on slang' (anag.) (but is all 15 Across so pure in speech?) (two words – 4,6)
8 Doing nothing because there's nothing doing possibly (4)
10 The kind of constitution that laughs at doctors of the Goebbels type! (10)
11 Our supposed portion in 1940, but we never tumbled to it . . . (4)
12 . . . though coming to the this of it (4)
15 Where the work of the architect stands very high (two words – 3,4)
18 The girl who went into her own reflections very amusingly (5)
19 You must be plumb right! (5)
20 Just a note (5)
21 Got in wrongly to the bar (5)
22 Would this problem be a sitter to an artist? (5)
23 A joint affair (5)
24 Not a forbidding hue (5)
25 She is in an ancient city (official!) (5)
26 Of Eastern origin, but serious (7)
30 Cast a skin (4)
33 Points in favour of some players? (4)
34 A submarine should be, of course (10)
35 He gets his wings on false pretences (4)
36 Where to look for Maud's boyfriend? (two words – 6,4)

DOWN

2 Sign of appeal to men (4)
3 Cause of the hidden hand? (5)
4 Like a bear with a sore head (5)
5 He may be like the curate's egg, good in parts (5)
6 Outcast agents of fickle chance (4)
7 Flower one might well salute (4)
9 End of a term for losing cohesion (two words – 8,2)

Leonard Sidney Dawe

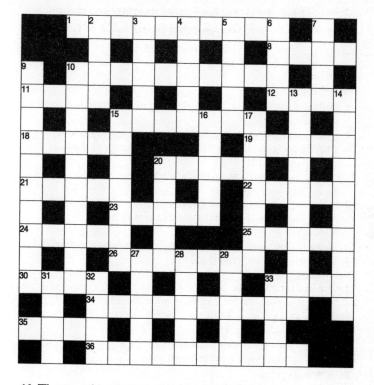

10 Those working in it are quite sunk in their work
(two words – 6,4)

13 It may be seen at the front at feeding time (two words – 5,5)

14 See printer for an adventure (10)

15 Britannia and he hold to the same thing (7)

16 Sphere of 15 Down (5)

17 An exclusive notice (two words – 4,3)

20 The root of smokers' pleasures (5)

27 It comes from the rates – blooming scandal! (5)

28 Choice of directions of tongue (5)

29 Was an arm, or might support one (5)

31 No good man will live up to it (4)

32 Shoot to spot (4)

33 Finished! (4)

41

11

11 July 1950: Pakistan joins the IMF and the International Bank

ACROSS

1 Not where one would meet plain people (9)

6 Where good-nights may be dryly said (5)

9 Shake-up that produces only a third of 18B allocation (9)

10 See the song is turned in fashion befitting a good subject (5)

11 The extent and nature of this depends on personal points, of course (9)

14 Dislocated joint underneath (5)

15 Given this, the dead heat is a certainty (4)

16 Given to mow around with the willow, it is obviously not Australia's cricket mascot (6)

19 To say he was himself might be a descriptive epitaph (5)

20 Smart at the ends, but unbefitting an orderly room (7)

22 Forced an entry with a bar? (5)

23 Foreign florin? (6)

24 Where there's a catch, how to get out of it (4)

26 Indian god (5)

27 Attic sham gives breathless results (9)

32 Breaking bail, I put up some defence (5)

33 'No A1 men up' (anag.) (all down with this?) (9)

34 To do so may make the list larger (5)

35 Is brown in repose, but not giving in easily (9)

DOWN

1 Ends of bee-lines (5)

2 There's too much talk at first in this part of the house (5)

3 Very little indeed to steal from (5)

4 One in the nose that effects the ears (5)

5 Reason to speak about some money turning up? (6)

6 A friend and a doctor each on an American shore (4,5)

7 Marine monarch makes an authoritative impression (5,4)

8 We try halo for what the church has blessed (4,5)

12 The parent whose children are usually in other people's clothes (4)

13 A supporter put up so appropriately (7)

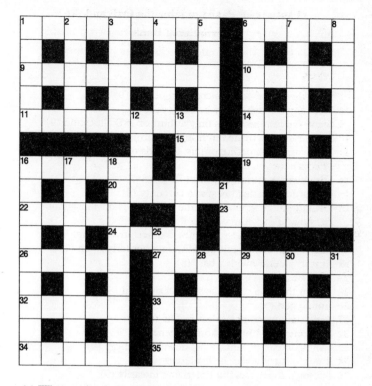

16 Where animals are not barred (9)
17 It certainly enables one to make the most of things
18 Concerning the work of one who calculates with assurance (9)
21 A gold-digger may have this in the first part of 6 Down (4)
25 This enables one to hold the initiative in draughts (6)
28 They should be well developed in the village blacksmith (5)
29 A swell thing to have (5)
30 This vehicle heartless used to be worn as a garment (5)
31 The ship that goes into making a ship (5)

12

13 January 1958: To mark the appearance of
the ten thousandth *Daily Telegraph* crossword puzzle
Leonard Dawe writes all the clues in rhyme

ACROSS

1, 18 & 33
Some celebration seems today in order;
So take your pen and let us now begin
The paper's first, the problem on the border,
And in between, its number; fill them in (5,10,3,10,9,6)

8 Has such journeying oft seemed short to you
Engaged in chasing the elusive clue? (5,6)

10 We only use him when we're in a jam
He wouldn't mind, he'd take it like a lamb! (4)

11 Fellows who polish up phrases, and toss them,
Crosswords can certainly 16 Across them (4)

13 As our good friend in need let his praises be sung
But his letters reveal he was born to be hung (1,1,1)

16 To this the lead, or boldly grasp the end?
Upon your solving skill that may depend (7)

17 Trail a red herring? We quite often do.
No need to follow – but that's up to you! (7)

18 See 1 Across

22 A mild deception or two's not amiss,
But you've never, we hope, thought us guilty of this (7)

24 Our aim's to intrigue, but fairly to treat you,
And never to try so completely to beat you (7)

25 Although he always fails and gives it up,
He's *proxime accessit* for the cup (3)

27 Wherein the make-up of a fly-by-night has started,
Although it's plain to see that father's not downhearted (4)

31 A seaside snap of it is a prize indeed,
But it's a close-up that you really need (4)

32 Time to relax; the paper to be read,
The puzzle to complete, and so to bed (7,4)

33 See 1 Across

Leonard Sidney Dawe

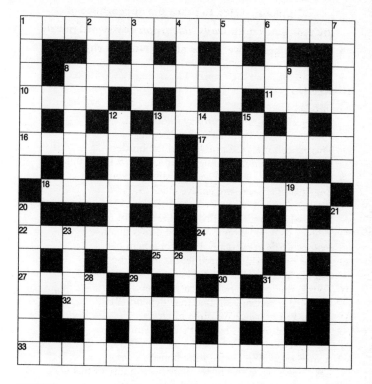

DOWN

1 We like to think that our efforts sometimes may
   Help speed its patient victim's tedious day (7)

2 Talking of 8 Across, the wanderlust's trail
   May lead you abroad, so here's cash for the rail (4)

3 Try to this you, sir or madam? No.
   Our aim's to elevate, not bring you low (4)

4 One may defer it oft when in doubt,
   And start to retaliate if put about (5)

5 At its pointed appeal
   Adds first half with zeal (4)

6 When your brain's a bit woolly, best give it a miss,
   Come back to it 4 Down, and tackle it this (4)

 7 From 1 Down comes this, for a holiday mood;
   When it rains it is better to puzzle than brood (7)

 8 Reproof your letters sometimes bring, and little doubt we need it,
   But when as vehement as this it's quite a change to read it! (6)

 9 Do you think we are clever? The point is a moot one;
   We dare not suggest so, not wanting to shoot one! (4)

12 Detected it, have you? Or are you still cool?
   It was placed before Dick as a pudding at school (7)

13 We use it in clues, fairly often indeed,
   But not many will help you to get what you need (7)

14 We hope you may find a clue, once in a while,
   That's sufficiently this to cause you to smile . . . (7)

15 . . . but we should indeed be most sadly remiss
   If we offered you efforts as foolish as this (7)

19 His chattering sometimes makes one yearn
   To give him cross words to return (6)

20 Why begin to show your grief of mind?
   It's secret, yes, but not too hard to find (7)

21 This nought, deceased the rest,
   But treat it as you would a pest (7)

23 To open one's mouth, as the foolish may do,
   Might provide a whole page, but that's all for this clue (4)

26 Just chance your arm, an adjective essay,
   Don't pick a bone with us if you're astray! (5)

28 This may be rare, a last-ditch sort of word,
   For which the compiler risks getting the bird! (4)

29 Most clues intrigue the mind, quotations don't.
   For guesses apart, you will this or you won't (4)

30 In their business some men walk it,
   Out of business others talk it (4)

31 What blew up here may bring us echoes yet,
   And one of the Olympics was upset! (4)

Douglas Barnard

Douglas Barnard arrived in England from Australia in 1954. He found himself a job as a freelance industrial consultant, and started to read the *Daily Telegraph* on a regular basis. He was rather taken with the cryptic crossword, and after a while reckoned he could do as good a job at creating them as the compilers used by the paper. So he sent an example of his work to the editor. The *Telegraph* was impressed, but needed confirmation that he could keep up this standard. They asked him to deliver another dozen puzzles within a week. He obliged on both counts. His puzzles were published on an occasional basis until Melville Jones (Leonard Dawe's co-compiler) retired in the mid-1950s, when Barnard became a regular *Telegraph* compiler. He created just under 3,000 puzzles for the paper, the final one appearing on 21 March 1994, two months before his death. Each puzzle was a jewel.

So what makes Douglas Barnard one of the greatest crossword compilers to grace the pages of the *Telegraph*? Firstly, he was mind-bogglingly clever, both in the conventional sense and, more importantly for a crossword compiler, in an unconventional, lateral way. And secondly, he was born at the right time.

Douglas Barnard was born in January 1924, making him eighteen months older than the *Daily Telegraph* crossword. Therefore, he had no back-history of riddles, conundrums and acrostics. By the time he first glanced at the *Telegraph* puzzle in 1954, it was a fully-fledged cryptic crossword – albeit one that had not properly stretched its wings. The wing-stretching was done by Barnard, who very quickly began turning out elegant, witty and beguiling crossword clues that (together with those of his fellow compiler Alan Cash) have never been bettered. His heyday was the 1960s and 1970s – particularly the latter decade – when his puzzles were sublime, as you will see from the examples in this book.

It was Barnard's nature that made him such a brilliant compiler – he was a clever, doughty, mischievous, irascible individual who was always wanting to push out the boundaries. He was forever trying to slip a questionable clue – i.e. one with a witty but shocking double entendre – past his crossword editor, i.e. me. And when he did, it was I not he who reaped the consequences. Quite early on in my crossword-editing career he came up with:

Clue: Burns 'em in boxes (8)
Solution: *Cremates*
*''em' inside 'crates' (boxes) giving CR-EM-ATES
or 'cremates'*

Clever, apposite clue, I murmured to myself and thought no more of it. Wrong! Not clever clue, but clue bent on causing offence. You would be astonished at the number of letters I got from people who had just had a loved one cremated and were deeply offended by that Barnard clue. It was an early lesson – just because a clue is clever does not mean it is going to appeal to solvers; sometimes other factors weigh in the balance.

But Barnard was a brilliant compiler, and it was his character that informed his brilliance, and what made his character was a life full of adversity overcome by sheer bloody-mindedness.

A clergyman's son and the youngest of five children, he was born at Pakefield, Suffolk, and christened Douglas St Paul Barnard. All his life he claimed the nomenclature 'Douglas St P. Barnard', but it wasn't until after his death I discovered that the 'St P.' stood for St Paul – he never let on. All three of his brothers became clergymen, so he probably felt there was enough religion in the family without his contribution!

Most of his early life was spent in Australia, where he was educated at the Brisbane Boys' College. In 1942, at the age of eighteen, he enlisted in the Australian army, fighting the Japanese on the Pacific front. Part of his service was spent in New Guinea, where – barely out of his teens – he wrote a book on pidgin English. Local chiefs assumed that, as an Englishman, Barnard was bound to be a friend of George VI, and one of them offered him the services of his wives.

At the end of the Second World War Barnard

transferred to the Army Psychology Corps, testing and interviewing discharged soldiers with a view to their civilian employment. It was at this time that he was brought to the attention of his employers, as he easily passed any psychological or intelligence tests put in front of him. Finally a test was produced for him alone, and he was put to work creating tests for others.

In 1946 he entered the University of Tasmania in Hobart to read political science. He failed to graduate, owing to expulsion, a distinction he shared with Errol Flynn, the 1940s and 50s film star, but for quite different reasons. Barnard had published a pamphlet denouncing a professor in the economics department as a communist. Three meetings of the professorial board demanded successively: a public apology and a fine; a public apology; and at the third meeting just a very small fine. All of these Barnard refused, by this time enjoying his public celebrity and determined not to yield one iota (as I said earlier, bloody-minded!). Barnard's main regret was forfeiting a Rhodes scholarship to study at Oxford.

Aged twenty-four, Barnard left university to join the Civil Service, the Commonwealth European Migration Scheme, to be precise, as officer in charge of migrant employment. It was in New South Wales in 1948 that he met his future wife, Dorcia Nowak, a Pole who worked in the reception camp as his secretary and interpreter. This was, he said, one of the happiest periods of his life – facing new challenges daily and meeting widely diverse people.

He was climbing high in the Civil Service and was rumoured to be in line for the job of secretary to the then prime minister, Robert Menzies, when in 1950 Barnard was struck with polio, which paralysed him for several months. Despite the specialist's prognosis that he would be unlikely to walk again, he designed his own leg clamp and succeeded, quite literally, in getting himself back on his feet. But for the rest of his life he had a limp in his right leg.

In 1957, three years after he and his wife moved to England (which he had always regarded as his true home), he moved to Cheltenham, where he lived as an author and freelance journalist until his death in 1994.

From 1957 to 1977 he contributed two cryptic puzzles a week to the *Daily Telegraph*; after 1977 it was just one a week – Friday's, the most cryptic and beguiling crossword of the week and one that solvers had to work up to in the previous four days. The *Daily Telegraph* was the only national newspaper he supplied with crosswords, but he wrote articles, under various pseudonyms, for more than twenty journals and scripted programmes for the BBC and ITV. In 1967 he compiled puzzles for the BBC2 programme *Crossword on Two*, a very tricky task, as he told me: 'The trouble is you have to create a crossword that a team of two or three can solve in 30 minutes – not 10 or 20 minutes but 30 minutes, and it *has* to be solvable in that time. Now that *is* difficult.' But he relished the challenge.

What made Barnard's puzzles special was his lightness of touch. He was a consummate polymath and could grasp the arcane details of any discipline – science, mathematics, religion, philosophy and computers were of particular interest. In the early days of computers he wrote his own program for compiling crosswords, so he had all the *Telegraph* patterns on file and the means to fill them with solution words.

At the same time he was also a craftsman who almost single-handedly rewired, replumbed and restored his large Georgian house in Cheltenham. He designed and built a large Adam-style mantelpiece, restored a Bechstein piano and collected and restored oriental porcelain. In 1964 he stood as Conservative candidate for West Gloucestershire – his pessimism about his chances of election were well founded.

All of these skills were summoned when it came to creating crossword clues. He was the Roger Federer of the crossword-compiling world – stunning ability made to look easy and elegant. Take his:

Clue: Bowing to advice on how to avoid
     peak-rate telephone charges (9)
Solution: *Deferring (defer ring)*

Perfect!
  Or:

Clue: Is it created by recession, little work,
     and a lout in the making? (4,10)
Solution: *Slum population*

> '*Slump*' *meaning recession and* '*op*' *meaning*
> *little work plus an anagram of* '*a lout in*' *giving*
> '*slump-op-ulation*' *or* '*slum population*', *which is*
> *defined by the whole clue* '*Is it created by recession,*
> *little work, and a lout in the making?*'

So deceptively simple and so fiendishly complicated. Genius! As close as you'll get in crossword terms to the Cirencester word-square mentioned in the introduction to this book.

And my all-time favourite:

Clue: *Twelfth Night or What You Will* after *Much*
  Ado About Nothing (7)
Solution: *Tiffany*

Please bear with me on this one because it's complicated. For a start, forget Shakespeare altogether. 'What you will' means 'any', and a 'tiff' is a petty argument or 'much ado about nothing'. If you put the word 'any' after the word 'tiff' you get 'tiff-any' or 'tiffany'. And now it gets even more complicated. Twelfth Night is 5 January, the eve of the twelfth day after Christmas or the Feast of the Epiphany. Tiffany is a thin, silk-like gauze: the word 'tiffany' is supposed to be a corruption of 'theophany' – the manifestation of God to man, the Epiphany – and the material was so called because it was worn at the Twelfth Night (Epiphany) revels. Now, I am willing to bet a pound to a penny that you didn't know that! But the *Telegraph* reader of thirty or forty years ago might well have known such things.

The 1960s and 70s were a world away from the present. It was a pre-digital, pre-computer age for the average person. Commercial television had only started in the mid-1950s, BBC2 didn't arrive until 1964 and colour television first flourished its rather garish hues in 1967. Television broadcasting stopped at about 11.30p.m. and youth danced the night away in clubs and discos – if they could afford it. The Sixties in London were 'swinging', as everyone on Planet Earth must know by now, but I was there and, believe me, it was all pretty tame compared to London 2008 – there was less booze, fewer drugs and a lot more culture.

Culture came, on the whole, from education – and that was both narrow and deep. In the 1950s and 60s the average *Telegraph* reader was probably grammar-school educated, 'reasonably well-read, with a reasonable knowledge of world affairs', as Miss M. R. K. Binstead put it, and she should know, as she was cross-word editor on the *Daily Telegraph* from the mid-1950s to the mid-1970s. To be reasonably well-read in the 1960s and 70s was a far cry from what it might mean now. It meant being conversant with the Greek and Roman myths, having read the classic English novelists – Dickens, Austen, Brontë (read them, *not* just watched the films!) – and Shakespeare, of course. You would also have some classic poetry committed to memory, a knowledge of history, including the dates of some main events, and most likely a smattering of Latin and music. And, more than likely, absolutely no knowledge of science, technology or much else. In a nutshell, a classic English mid-twentieth-century grammar-school education.

You think I am exaggerating? I well remember that in 1977 a new compiler incorporated the solution 'Close Encounters of the Third Kind' into her crossword. It was Steven Spielberg's global smash-hit sci-fi film that year, but I still had one or two *Telegraph* crossword solvers bitterly complaining that we should never have used it, as they had certainly never heard of this film.

However, back to Barnard's clues:

Clue: Convince the electorate it's the only way to vote (3,6)
Solution: *Put across (put a cross – geddit?)*

Clue: Sportsman who provides hospital recreation facilities (6,7)
Solution: *Centre forward (centre for ward)*

Clue: Making patterns on metal, glass, etc., with an ache (4)
Solution: *Etch*
It took me a little while to solve this one – I didn't have the answers to hand so it was down to solving. The solution had to be 'etch', but why? Then the penny dropped: it's not 'ache' pronounced ayck *meaning pain, but 'ache' pronounced* aitch *meaning the letter 'h', which, put after the 'etc.' in the clue, gives 'etc-h' or 'etch' or 'making patterns on metal, glass . . .'*

Clue: Both hungry for the election vote (5)
Solution: *Booth*
*'Both' with nothing – '0' (zero) – inside it, i.e.
'hungry', making 'bo-0-th' or 'booth', which is
used for an election vote.*

You needed wit, intelligence and humour to solve
Barnard's clues, and he needed wit, intelligence and
humour to create them for *Telegraph* solvers. It was a
match made in a cruciverbalist's heaven.

Incidentally, when I reduced Barnard's output to a
mere one puzzle a week, he insisted that he be compen-
sated with something else to make up for the financial
loss. He was freelance and the loss of a crossword a week
was significant. Barnard was indefatigable in argument,
and being berated with cogent reasons for another
puzzle by someone who was a dead ringer for Captain
Birds Eye in the TV ads soon wore me down. So from
1978 onwards he produced for the Saturday paper a
'Brain Twister' – a weekly reasoning problem, sometimes logical, sometimes mathematical and sometimes
linguistic, but always witty. For a decade he produced
one a week until ill health forced him to concentrate on
crosswords.

He also wrote books, including *Adventures in Mathematics*, *It's All Done by Numbers*, *Figure It Out* and,
probably one of the greatest books on cruciverbalism,
Anatomy of the Crossword.

I will leave the last word on Barnard to Barnard
– his words at *the end* of his book *Anatomy of the*

Crossword are as true now as they were then. And, after reading them, enjoy his puzzles.

It is strange that in a world beset by real problems of inescapable clamancy, man should choose to set himself still more problems in the form of patterns and clues. Perhaps it is a sign of human perversity. On the other hand it may be that he finds it a welcome change to grapple occasionally with some challenge which, unlike so many of the world's problems, really can be met – something which really has got an answer, and can be solved – to the very letter – something from which one *can* draw:

A definite conclusion (3,3).

13

20 March 1956: Tunisia gains independence

ACROSS

1 The badger-dog (9)
8 There is trouble ahead and a debt to settle (3,5,2,3)
11 A warning is nothing to the fellows (4)
12 Facilitate entry, perhaps, in the gun-barrel (5)
13 A mud concoction from old Russia (4)
16 Delight with more than a song (7)
17 It has horns and I'm lamed (7)
18 Bald as a Cockney and finding it close (7)
20 Feel sick at heart; here's total weakness (7)
21 A happy thought from 2 Down (4)
22 Loud vessel for not so many (5)
23 A foreign river-valley but not much river usually (4)
26 In it one reputedly enjoys the greatest bliss (7,6)
27 This, of course, comes later than 5 Down (9)

DOWN

2 The attendant who may decamp without punishment (4)
3 The Avon is a poor thing (4-3)
4 Seek it in the Netherlands, and finish there (7)
5 Time for onions but is not here (4)
6 This kind of fight in politics is not a straight affair (5-8)
7 There is nothing in the first part, but the whole cleans up (6,7)
9 The home of a little dog (9)
10 To kill haphazardly in a foreign capital brings things to immobility (9)
14 Shelter to get to if you possess the direction (5)
15 Young Florence at a buoyant affair (5)
19 Even if not believed in, it might be a source of respect (7)
20 24 Down comes back with poultry to put new life in one (7)
24 One might expect to hear this drudge sound on the beach (4)
25 A Manx cat with the quality of a Censor (4)

Douglas Barnard

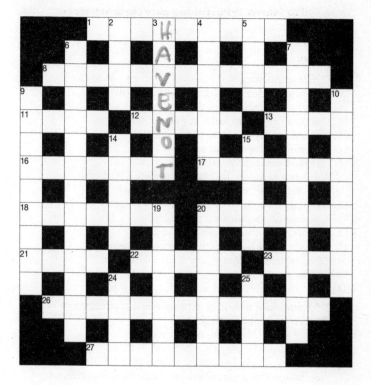

14

18 March 1959: Hawaii becomes the fiftieth state of the USA

ACROSS

1 A grim association with the not-so-young flower (8)
5 Things to be done with time and change (6)
9 Being reluctant to put money on a regressive draw (8)
10 The trick of being French in place of English (6)
12 Men often follow it for those who load ships (9)
14 A huge following stop at sea (5)
15 Returned many as quite dismal (3)
16 You will find me in the money, hardly set (6)
19 With IOUs this becomes deficient in interest (5)
22 It's customary (5)
23 Rare, indeed, is much of this poison (6)
25 A bit of positive advice gives trouble (3)
28 Our race but it would be kind to put it to the East (5)
29 Castle armament? (4-5)
32 Get the boat in, it's a wreck! (6)
33 Might the motorist term it top cover? (8)
34 Maybe a four-minute man about fifty is a corny fellow (6)
35 He expects some interest from you when he presents his account (8)

DOWN

1 Prophet turns against the crowd, easily moved (6)
2 Tear round the City postal area and still be fresh (6)
3 The dresses G— possesses? (5)
4 Handel produced it in slow time (5)
6 Soldier once engaged in a sort of bomb disposal (9)
7 A troublesome thing is in a shade of difference (8)
8 An opening for a cameraman (8)
11 One who tries to make a coin (6)
13 Not a first-rate actor; one may even associate him with eggs! (3)
17 Plant in a gentle arrangement (9)
18 The call of success? (6)
20 The shape of fearful clouds, gathered in the morning (8)
21 A constituent of many barrels (8)

Douglas Barnard

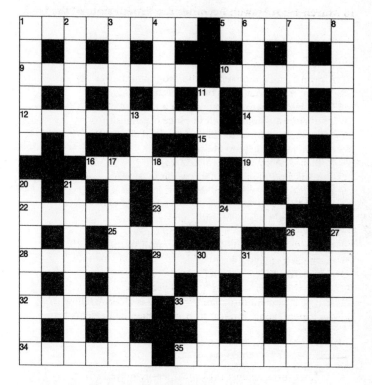

24 One-time home for animals in the market (3)
26 Produce the result of an action (6)
27 A close comparison proves less generous (6)
30 The last word in Greece? (5)
31 However one looks at it, impulse and reflection must play a signal part in this (5)

15

ACROSS

1 Maybe the French siren's song for the trader (8)
5 A fat lot of good, one who is always raising objections (6)
9 Bird-song to summon school back (4-4)
10 Climbs on the piano possibly (6)
11 War doctor gets a decoration and it will doubtless suit him (8)
12 Morning employed in being entertained it would seem (6)
14 To which candidates choose to speak at length (10)
18 Meeting one of the requirements of polite society (10)
22 The General Assembly in session? Let's hope the members
   will be able to act in it! (6)
23 Fish, as many do in deep water (8)
24 A prohibition including the District Attorney in Iran (6)
25 Retiring debutante gets dates mixed up, perhaps she should
   sleep on it (8)
26 Time they should start play at the Oval? (6)
27 Graduate returns to supply the means, not being stubborn (8)

DOWN

1 Up river was a confusion of parrots (6)
2 Liners carrying them are usually escorted (6)
3 European country sustains a loss, needing food (6)
4 A well-known person maybe, but presumably lacking in skill
   (10)
6 A French colonel with a British decoration on is quite unusual
   (8)
7 The most charming of Sir Walter Scott's novels? (8)
8 Revised, reissued remainders (8)
13 Its end always entails some breaking up (6,4)
15 A note to the lowly parson should be all correct (8)
16 Imagine it's in the French face! (8)
17 The little editor turns up so much after time, and quite forlorn
   (8)
19 A British explorer on the run through New York State (6)
20 It modifies part of speech and could be braved (6)
21 A way across for the game (6)

Douglas Barnard

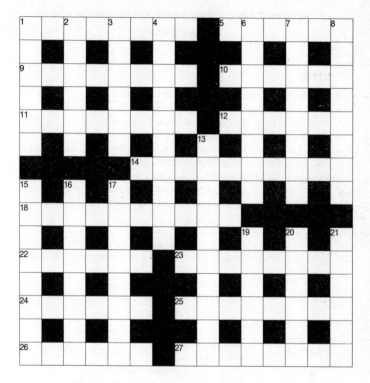

16

19 October 1966: Aftershocks of the earthquake and tsunami in Peru

ACROSS

8 One skilled in the fine arts? O, very! (8)
9 Most so-called little devils are, really (3,3)
10 Measuring stick often used at an angle (3)
11 Military cover in buff we hear? (8)
12 Turncoat showing hesitation at the pithead (6)
13 Primarily where a leader should be (2,3,5,5)
15 He may have to sit out until required, however (5-2)
18 In which many have found a watery grave, no doubt (4,3)
21 Factotum with a coloured staff in Spain? (6,2,7)
24 Show up a noisy party outside (6)
25 Blunt 26 remodelled for chewing in the East (5-3)
26 One steps on it, of course, to drive off (3)
27 Prohibit an article that's very fruity! (6)
28 Opening for a photographer (8)

DOWN

1 Glutton taking a long time gets the bird (6)
2 Stiff preparation for Jack in the little school (6)
3 A hard and sweet memento of a topical bone of contention? (4,2,9)
4 Hide-outs familiar to stock controllers, no doubt (7)
5 Indisposed as high-fliers seldom are (5,3,7)
6 Put a foot wrong, by chance (8)
7 Hanger-on instrumental in pacifying a horse (8)
14 A plant that is usually potted (3)
16 The government's idea is to squeeze it together! (5,3)
17 He sounds a good member of his class (8)
19 Shining example of a Latin-American monetary unit (3)
20 Rhythm of the policeman, at the station? (3-4)
22 Marine arms, silent fashion (6)
23 Wherein a knowledge of art may be ventilated? (6)

Douglas Barnard

17

**11 November 1968: Start of the Vietnam War's
Operation Commando Hunt, by the end of which 3 million
tons of bombs have been dropped on Laos**

ACROSS

1 Is he out of breath from running up prices? (6)
4 A rolling stone, though the very epitome of statuesque
immobility (6)
10 Sort of annuity which could be divided into ten (7)
11 The best policy for those who like permanent flower
arrangements? (7)
12 A way out of advice to the pools enthusiast who thinks the
match will be drawn (4)
13 Jump the gun? (5)
14 Card game devoid of harmony? (4)
17 It may be a headache, but is not quite the same as the pink
variety! (5,8)
18 Hardly suitable refreshment for guests needing a square meal
(5,2,6)
23 Many are usually drawn (4)
24 The prize of which sister takes charge (5)
25 Dismal sportsman (4)
28 Note the slow moving horse; the one who backs (7)
29 The list which gives one 9 divided by 150 (7)
30 Whist player's combination which is a natural for the pontoon
player (6)
31 A short line of music by all accounts (6)

DOWN

1 A succession of taps for comic use (6)
2 Language, the pronunciation of which would seem conclusive
(7)
3 Live up to what one may later have to live down (4)
5 If her name is Sally she is sure to be shy (4)
6 What final year arts students hope to be in the orchestra (7)
7 Of primary importance in grammar, it shows my rise in school
(6)
8 Sportsman who provides hospital recreation facilities? (6,7)

Douglas Barnard

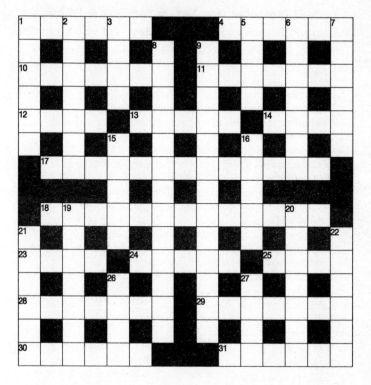

9 Raw as children might be, he described their genetic variations (7,6)
15 Its centre is 160 times the weight of its whole (5)
16 It is linked with surveying (5)
19 Motto put up over an oriental (7)
20 What makes the princely ruler turn sick at heart? (7)
21 Hardly a big insult (6)
22 Highlight said to be from Christopher Robin's appointments book? (6)
26 Home for a smart lad (4)
27 Area in which care should be used (4)

18

ACROSS

1 Bring in a worker of some consequence (9)
8 Single armies prepared to appeal to their leader (13)
11 Non-fliers from the Middle East backed by America (4)
12 Both hungry for the election vote (5)
13 To pound back will result in a black mark (4)
16 Many set free! (7)
17 If twisted it naturally makes a chatter! (7)
18 Suppose I have silver in a mine (7)
20 Fruit found around an Indian mountain provides food generally (7)
21 Make patterns on metal, glass, etc., with an ache (4)
22 Beast right in a Scottish isle (5)
23 How to make one's name, or come to notice (4)
26 End the act in response to the highwayman? (5,3,5)
27 Marksman who apparently breaks under the strain (5,4)

DOWN

2 The air in Amiens (4)
3 Not exclusively Socialist speech (7)
4 Jenny is not one to be relied upon (7)
5 One's tweaked feature (4)
6 Further engagements, probably on different grounds (6,7)
7 Tiny grips for growing places (5,8)
9 Unfavourable responses for example in the indigenous population (9)
10 Tent mates contrive to make an announcement (9)
14 Now awake to what the Christmas pudding needs (5)
15 Strikes toe against one vessel enclosed in another (5)
19 Irregular deserter captured by Farrar's boy hero (7)
20 People who place things in position for golf clubs (7)
24 A parson rises to assert the truth (4)
25 It smells two-thirds blotto (4)

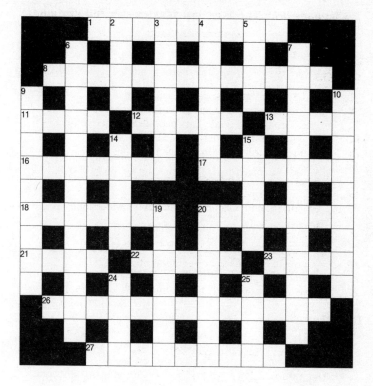

19

16 September 1977: Talking Heads release their debut album

ACROSS

1 Irish county prison warder is nothing but a crooked twister (9)
9 Neighbour who is a fat lot of good (7)
10 Winners needed for rousing game (7)
11 Her last change in old Germany (7)
12 Presumably it is admirably suited for planting bulbs in (5,4)
14 They were jolly well devoted to Robin (5,3)
15 Irish Johnny takes Anglican to spiritual revival meeting (6)
17 Speech which may be written down for delivery (7)
20 Was garden partly assigned to dead heroes? (6)
23 Current notice displayed on vehicle behind breakdown truck (8)
25 Upon a mine explosion it adversely affects the lungs (9)
26 Tree containing variety of lac which is edible but sticky (7)
27 Wayward son involved in strikes gets payments for life (7)
28 Notice old boy has to start the tennis match (7)
29 Bowing to advice on how to avoid peak-rate telephone charges (9)

DOWN

2 Once once (3-4)
3 Urge to be in the know where fare is put up (7)
4 Being taken in by a joker maybe – an amorous one it would seem (8)
5 Fencing for power and left a foot short (6)
6 Convince the electorate it's the only way to vote (3,6)
7 Masters involved in selective education? (7)
8 Objected to under a penny being given (9)
13 Obscure way Tom identified himself to Dr Arnold (7)
15 Work place (9)
16 Tropic isle the footsore should go to (9)
18 Soak took a seat with a true flourish (8)
19 Contrary to part of what must be a Christian hymn (7)
21 Does he complain if he can't get 10 on the twelfth? (7)
22 Trainer ran around dilapidated Peruvian capital (7)
24 Prepared to read circular letter writer supplied to the editor (6)

20

ACROSS

1 The man's no Whig, but that's all past (7)
5 Wilde flower? (4)
9 Maritime company ass replaces any ship's instrument (8,7)
10 Surprised expression of a pair struck by an afterthought (4)
11 Concerned with permanent loss of pools system (5)
12 160 square poles taken by 1192 crusaders (4)
15 Gave the waiter about a pound when boozed (7)
16 Carbon chain raked from a cold furnace? (7)
17 Loudly announce decision of militant strike committee (4,3)
19 Baby caterpillar tractor (7)
21 An expletive which should be taken seriously (4)
22 Frequently decimal (5)
23 Pans right to left for a quick camera shot (4)
26 Junk going for a song (4,4,2,5)
27 Play loud instead of soft. Skinners do just that (4)
28 Don't follow suit – refuse (7)

DOWN

1 Striking teacher's demand for the dole? (4,3)
2 Is it created by recession, little work, and a lout in the making?
(4,10)
3 Don't include sex appeal which follows order of merit (4)
4 Longed for twelve months over Kelly (7)
5 Brief airman on internal combustion (7)
6 The French feminine doctor who became an essayist (4)
7 He proposed milk of a purest form (7)
8 The Shrove Tuesday art resorted to by a desperate aviator
(7,7)
13 Concede that none suffers in silence (5)
14 I'm upset, upset, upset, despite my golden handshake! (5)
17 Thwarted by being marked wrong (7)
18 *Twelfth Night or What You Will* after *Much Ado About Nothing* (7)
19 City represented by Conservative supported by Lady
Stanhope (7)

Douglas Barnard

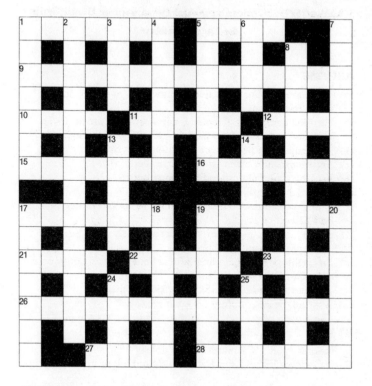

20 Substitute coarse fabric by far more delicate stuff (7)
24 First man to be murdered and pronounced fit (4)
25 Third of the Scandinavian survey (4)

21

11 May 1987: The first heart–lungs transplant is performed by Dr Bruce Reitz

ACROSS

1 Human merriment means robbing others of their living (12)
9 Continuous at the time of departure (7)
10 For Catholics in 1673 it was a setback needing diplomacy (4,3)
11 Look noble (4)
12 Returnable note (5)
13 A pointed reminder of galactic immensity (4)
16 Cut off a confession of extreme tardiness (7)
17 Adherence to accepted code involves breaking the code – how odd! (7)
18 Given permission to leave former spouse about to be employed (7)
21 I'd turn to a geometric proposition for a very difficult problem (7)
23 Lebanese town blown up after it is flat (4)
24 Worsted, despite a pronounced surge (5)
25 Use a mess of pottage? To whom was that question put? (4)
28 Reagan's pronouncement on SDI weaponry (3,4)
29 It sums up 2.71828 by 3.14159 by volume (7)
30 Glowing genealogical report on pure-blooded Peruvian (12)

DOWN

1 Attractive bar has appeal for current generation (7)
2 Return article if it is too unsophisticated (4)
3 It is put into a new ingle, and there burned (7)
4 Green still on remand? (7)
5 One who entertains a great number of people (4)
6 He no longer plays any role except that of Shylock? (7)
7 Sort of kind remark that is just the ticket for a deadhead (13)
8 Harsh treatment assures me rent collection (13)
14 Pastoral accommodation means reconstruction (5)
15 Climb on the reptile's back, maybe (5)
19 Continue with food for crows, from the sound of it (5,2)
20 What soldiers of the line did fully clothed (7)

Douglas Barnard

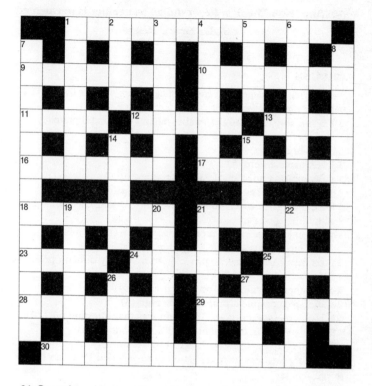

21 Stray American serviceman turns up in female attire (7)
22 Lose one's chance, when calling to see the young lady (4,3)
26 Fish upsets a crazy fellow (4)
27 Escape tool for one serving life? (4)

22

ACROSS

1 Dramatic scenes put on by myopics (10)
9 Insect chewed up leaf (4)
10 Presumably he's wedded to the soil (10)
11 Slippery way to bribe (6)
12 Felt sad for first woman caught in grating (7)
15 Listen to rumours (7)
16 Songs that echo? (5)
17 Bill goes to Yorkshire area with adolescent complaint (4)
18 New star Avon turned back (4)
19 What the oyster has to face (5)
21 Died before five with debts clear (7)
22 Held up amateur caught in the act (7)
24 Attack the bowling? (3,3)
27 Choose to lecture the voters (10)
28 Unauthorized retreat (4)
29 Carriage to drive mad around the harbour (10)

DOWN

2 Stop advertising (4)
3 Repair a sole paving stone (6)
4 First letter sorts out knots for relations (7)
5 Walk as though stiff, though not stiff (4)
6 Tickets for a Wimbledon match maybe (7)
7 What investigative reporter might do with an upper floor (5-5)
8 Produced by employee, but not mass produced (4,2,4)
12 Revolutionary music maker (10)
13 Local applause is something new (10)
14 In old Venice top dogs swallowed earth (5)
15 What the miser had or collected (5)
19 Barrel tip or opposite part of a rifle (4,3)
20 Wildly berated his opponent he did (7)
23 Worker on edge in Ireland (6)
25 Look both ways (4)
26 School which teaches point to point (4)

23

ACROSS

1 Volume of dispensable products (13)
10 One who knows a trick or two used cards (3,4)
11 Showed patience in the interests of a tedious fellow (7)
12 Not a figure of speech from the sort of Esperanto
 followed by 50 (4)
13 Solve the latest drug problem (5)
14 Appeal to Henry over the head of a saintly figure (4)
17 Obtain fluffy feathers from duck (3,4)
18 Carrots for Mr Gorbachev (7)
19 Try in parliament to get one parliamentarian
 everyone follows (7)
22 Hot drink now converted to steam? (7)
24 Deserve to make money (4)
25 Fish had apparently been left too long! (5)
26 Insubstantial nest (4)
29 Not an ethnic problem which has completely
 disappeared (2,5)
30 To study the journey get a line on the map (7)
31 Smoker in church (7,6)

DOWN

2 Retreat if tanning is being done in the open air (4-3)
3 Bore out a pile of paper (4)
4 Rest of the firewood and metal (7)
5 Propose about one cent for a recipient of commission (7)
6 Claim we make calls for lots of time (4)
7 Cut off a confession of extreme unpunctuality (7)
8 Lofty messengers (6,7)
9 The highest scoring sportsmen who only reproduce
 the score? (6,7)
15 Decayed molar teaches one a lesson (5)
16 Melancholy resulting from a perpetual household
 problem (5)
20 Train up in a way that makes for a prudish character (7)

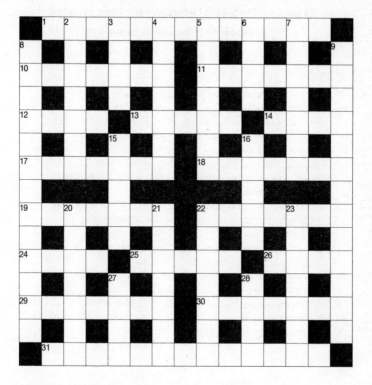

21 Holds up picnic baskets (7)
22 West gets club of suit for one of the pack (4-3)
23 Famous school invested in unbeatable service and is solvent (7)
27 Crippled but plucky (4)
28 Nero contrived to be a remarkable person (4)

24

**16 November 1992: Bill Clinton starts his first week as
president of the United States**

ACROSS

1 Lost interest when the matter was postponed (3,3)
4 Highly satisfactory method is quite some distance off
(1,4,3)
9 Utter base calumny then hide (3,3)
10 Joker gets firm to adopt a middle line (8)
12 Famous contralto, the object of jokes . . . (4)
13 . . . not stale, but impudent (5)
14 Fair pronouncement of one's doom (4)
17 Outpouring of this week's magazine (7,5)
20 Penny game enough to suffer the discomforts of
sea travel (5,3,4)
23 Parched terrorists returned and then died (4)
24 Where I'm backing Bradman to hit the ball? (3,2)
25 Plea to woman to give orphan sanctuary (4)
28 Not a bad prison for healthy people to be in (4,4)
29 In days the Federalist dream falls to pieces (6)
30 He should provide a cue with less delay (8)
31 Brother Baker is devastated (6)

DOWN

1 Check a racehorse, place a bet, and retire (4,4)
2 They make films best seen through telescopic lenses (3,5)
3 Sell birch (4)
5 Complain over pepper and salt from August to December
(6,6)
6 Ancient thorn in Australia started the old town crying (4)
7 In war I have made a renunciation (6)
8 One dry cocktail over there (6)
11 The Northern Line? (6,6)
15 Cotton on is the way to acquire sex appeal (3,2)
16 Damn'd healthy looking (5)
18 Quick reply by return (4,4)
19 In the same way clandestine troops wrong a murderous type
(8)

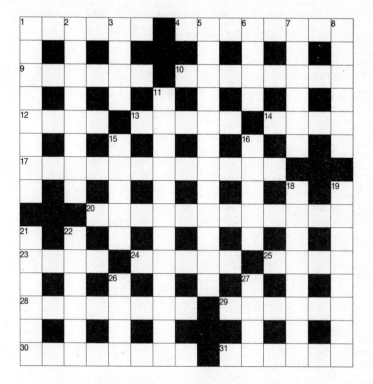

21 To bang down the phone indicates an emotional problem (4,2)
22 Jungle boy has nothing on but an Eastern robe (6)
26 Cut-price bargain? (4)
27 Equipment changed by motorists (4)

Alan Cash

When the founder-compiler of the *Daily Telegraph* crossword, Leonard Dawe, died in January 1963, it really was a case of 'the king is dead, long live the king'. And as 1963 progressed it became clear that 'Cash was king' in all senses.

Not only did Alan Cash, at the ripe old age of forty-seven, pull the crossword equivalent of Excalibur from the stone (in the pre-computer 1960s newspaper pages were set on an imposing 'stone' before being printed), compiling three superb crosswords each week for the *Daily Telegraph*, but he also proved the crossword crucial to the finances of the paper. In the mid-1960s a survey showed that 15 per cent of the *Daily Telegraph*'s readership took the paper for the crossword and a further 15 per cent gave it as a secondary reason – the readership in those days was some 3 million, which meant that at least a million people were regularly tackling the puzzle. Cash, indeed, was king.

So who was Alan Cash, and how did he become the *Telegraph* crossword's mainstay for twenty-five years, earning the title 'Grand Master' of British crosswords?

With the gift of hindsight, one can see that Cash and *Telegraph* crossword solvers were made for each other. He was a self-educated man, who became a school teacher. Charming and self-effacing, he was a stocky provincial Englishman – the epitome of what would appeal to the paper's solvers.

Solvers liked the simplicity of his puzzles – a preponderance of anagrams and straightforward cryptic clues, if that's not a contradiction in terms. While his fellow compiler Douglas Barnard would metaphorically stand in the corner with his arms folded, waiting, with a twinkle in his eye, for solvers to trip over his clues, Alan Cash would take them gently by the hand and show them the way. His passions were quintessentially English – history, cricket, literature – all the things that most of his solvers also knew about and loved.

Alan Cash was a Black Country man and proud of it. He was born in Darlaston, Staffordshire, in 1915 and educated at Wednesbury High School, where he first started compiling crosswords. The interest was instilled by his mother, who contributed puzzles to local newspapers.

At fifteen he had his first crossword published, in the *Daily Mirror*, printed under a neighbour's name, as it was thought he might be considered too young. He left school the following year, and two years later was compiling puzzles regularly for the *Birmingham Post* and the *News Chronicle*. He took a University of London correspondence course for an external degree in English, history and German. 'I'm afraid I neglected to send the work back regularly,' he told a friend. 'They once pointed this out and asked if there was any difficulty. I told them I had been busy doing crosswords and they said I should take the course more seriously!' He got a first – one of the very few awarded that year. He became a teacher, but was soon swept up in the Second World War, serving in North Africa, Italy and Austria as an interpreter and interrogator.

He told me of compiling crosswords in his tent at night by the light of a hurricane lamp in the North African desert. I can imagine him hunched over the paper, a study in concentration, sucking the end of a stub of pencil in the semi-darkness to the counterpoint of gunfire. A pleasing contrast to the shenanigans over Dieppe and D-Day code words taking place back at the *Telegraph*.

It was through his war work in Italy that he met his wife, Enrica; they were married in Padua and then lived with his father in Darlaston for four years. Enrica at that point spoke no English, but Alan included her in conversations with friends by rapidly translating everything into Italian – he was a brilliant linguist. In fact, he was a very clever man, having learned to read by the age of three, but extremely modest with it. He used to say that his standard method of dealing with problems was to do nothing. 'It usually works!'

On his return to England and the Black Country, he started teaching at Wednesbury Commercial College, and in 1950 the Cashes – now with two small daughters – moved to a large Victorian terraced house in Wednesbury, barely two miles from where he was born, which he considered home for the rest of his life. However, there was a period of three years in India. In 1952 he and his family left drab, post-war Britain for Bombay, where he organized competitions and crosswords for the *Illustrated Weekly of India* and the *Times of India.*

After the Indian interlude, he taught liberal studies at Cannock Mining College, but continued compiling crosswords. When he joined the *Telegraph* team in 1963, his crosswords had appeared in newspapers and magazines all over the world. In 1966 he gave up teaching to become a full-time crossword compiler. He said that he felt he could make a reasonably comfortable living without stirring from the fireside – and, of course, it would be easier to attend cricket matches at his beloved Worcestershire cricket club or mid-week theatre performances at Stratford. He was a great one for the eighteenth-century philosophy of unhurried living – speed was the curse of modern life, he believed.

But his output belied his words. Sitting in the front room of his house with his beloved cat Horace by his side, Cash produced a huge amount of work, creating the Saturday prize crossword and one or two others each week for the *Daily Telegraph*, and weekly puzzles for the *Scotsman*, the *Birmingham Post*, *Argosy* as well as books of crosswords for both Penguin and Puffin, the latter specially designed to interest nine- to thirteen-year-olds in crosswords and, until his death, editing the *Daily Telegraph* crossword books.

I am not quoting any of Cash's clues because the beauty of his work is in the whole puzzle, not individual clues – as pleasing and elegant as they are. Back in the mid-1960s, my mother was an avid *Telegraph* crossword solver and she really looked forward to the Saturday prize puzzle. She told me it was like sitting down with an old friend to discuss things that you both agreed over. 'I know it will make me smile and I should be able to finish it, and if I don't finish it, it is my own fault,' she told me. She never posted off the completed solution; she wasn't interested in winning a prize, just in solving the puzzle on a Saturday morning over a cup of tea. This was the marvellous strength of Cash's puzzles; they were the cruciverbalist's equivalent of the Mini car – stylish, reliable and lovable. They made you feel comfortable and in charge of things. Where Barnard's clues would dazzle you, Cash's crosswords would be in your comfort zone, cajoling the solutions out of your brain.

He was a literate man with an enormous library – his Wednesbury house filled up with hardback books over the course of the thirty-nine years he lived there. But his greatest strength was his humanity. A friend of his remembers passing a Salvation Army hostel which a number of old men were entering for their night's rest. 'They are all little Lears,' Cash said. 'I expect they were persuaded to give up their homes and live with a son or daughter, and it hasn't worked out.'

When Cash ran a weekly series of special crosswords for the *Birmingham Post*, he chose the sobriquet Autolycus, a character in Shakespeare's *The Winter's Tale*, who describes himself as 'a snapper-up of unconsidered trifles'. I hope Cash's twelve trifles give you a lot of pleasure – they should.

25

**6 February 1965: Seven GIs killed in a Vietcong raid on
a US base in Pleiku**

ACROSS

1 Cart-horses ordered to form harmonious groups (10)
9 He clowns always in a calico costume (4)
10 A proportion of buttons distributed around the centre, roughly (10)
11 Reputedly a great hunter, and not half nimble with the rod, too! (6)
12 A grizzled old time-server, the goose! (7)
15 Give back, or once more keep for future use? (7)
16 He has a gift for elasticity presumably! (5)
17 Glimpse among the snakes pythons in fact (4)
18 Uncertain pleasure (4)
19 A poet inspired by his native runners? (5)
21 No age is fitting for such great bodily sufferings (7)
22 Scattered in Kent, we hear (7)
24 Exempt from a particular kind of ill-feeling perhaps (6)
27 All novel characters are claimed to be, at the outset (10)
28 A queen from Iran (4)
29 'I can resist everything except ——' (Wilde) (10)

DOWN

2 Wind up with a most unpleasant look! (4)
3 For beginners it's bully off and on with the game! (6)
4 A form of military protection that could yet hit hard (4-3)
5 Twenty choirs sound enough for hundreds of letters! (4)
6 Stephen the poet, apparently no niggard (7)
7 'Wolf our cat' (anag.) (and you'll pay the penalty in it, perhaps!) (5,2,3)
8 Not a bad return for information to property-seekers? (4,6)
12 They could make green raids, but doubtless prefer to be in the red! (10)
13 Many choose to work solely through this agency, at least temporarily (10)
14 Suitable headgear in a theatre crush presumably (5)
15 Progress-checkers of power-units? (5)

19 Match which should do a veteran good (7)
20 He is expert at figures, being mostly a statistician (7)
23 Sign on for uniform 13 Down (6)
25 Dross part of Wordsworth's Cumberland (4)
26 She was a 'venerable and ox-eyed' deity, to the Romans (4)

26

ACROSS

1 Labels stocked in a different way (7)
5 Some light supporting feature, maybe (4)
9 A position that can't altogether be defended (10,5)
10 Not a regular military flight! (4)
11 Make one's own building supplement? (5)
12 'Tears, —— tears, I know not what they mean' (Tennyson: *The Princess*) (4)
15 A team always ahead of Continental fashion (7)
16 Had no bite, presumably (7)
17 A hermit sitting down to make notes? (7)
19 Some witchery that is fallible, apparently (7)
21 It causes fear by holding back leave (4)
22 Turned out fresh plays (5)
23 A brand to gain, perhaps (4)
26 It will be a capital play-centre when its finally ready! (8,7)
27 Relay no article to trust (4)
28 Anger restrained by a Mercian 14 Down borne aloft in triumph (7)

DOWN

1 Not like poetry I'd taken up to start with (7)
2 Traffic-signals seen by dazed pugilists! (8,6)
3 A vessel we bring up with little hesitation (4)
4 Contrasting points about a famous Carthaginian river (7)
5 Logs to keep the soldiers warm? (7)
6 High and mighty foreign playground (4)
7 Superior installations of mine (7)
8 The fakir on his bed of nails furnishes an example of its triumph! (4,4,6)
13 Short way to dry a step (5)
14 He does no wrong in dividing the last day (5)
17 It can be made into a powerful instrument of government (7)
18 The first woman hymnist? (7)
19 Lacking any order (7)

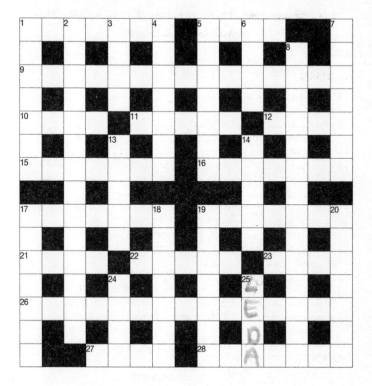

20 Claim to see to in advance? (7)
24 Pacific flier (4)
25 New deal for Helen's mother (4)

27

ACROSS

1 Booby prize for a good mixer! (6,5)
9 Port part of the ship (4)
10 The burglar's farewell! (5-6)
11 Not often, not now (4)
14 They are not human though, in a way, man ails for them (7)
16 Once beleaguered city having fortune this time (7)
17 So the characteristic spirit of the people has changed (5)
18 Organization needed in an atomic age (4)
19 His father must have raised Cain! (4)
20 Brass ones might be doubly unpopular at weddings (5)
22 A call to the late riser? (5,2)
23 A truest use to find height (7)
24 Part of the garden on the bishop's arms (4)
28 To begin with, one and one beside will make a good time (5,6)
29 A feature, we hear, of divisions (4)
30 Grammatical gooseberry, perhaps (5,6)

DOWN

2 Finished, the umpire cries (4)
3 A large number I've followed to take the plunge (4)
4 Unfit to be a bigwig? (7)
5 Jack's old-time weapon (4)
6 Bonus I'm getting for transport (7)
7 Fast colour? Yes, and no (7,4)
8 A dreamy type, unsuited to take a leap in the dark! (5-6)
12 Good lady Napoleon could have done without (5,6)
13 A musical catering for widely differing tastes (6-5)
15 Security device that breaks up? (5)
16 Another place for cricket enthusiasts (5)
20 Stock Exchange's rising (7)
21 Feed the fires (5,2)
25 Sure to upset the consumer (4)
26 Not far off being niggardly (4)
27 Nothing on the scales (4)

Alan Cash

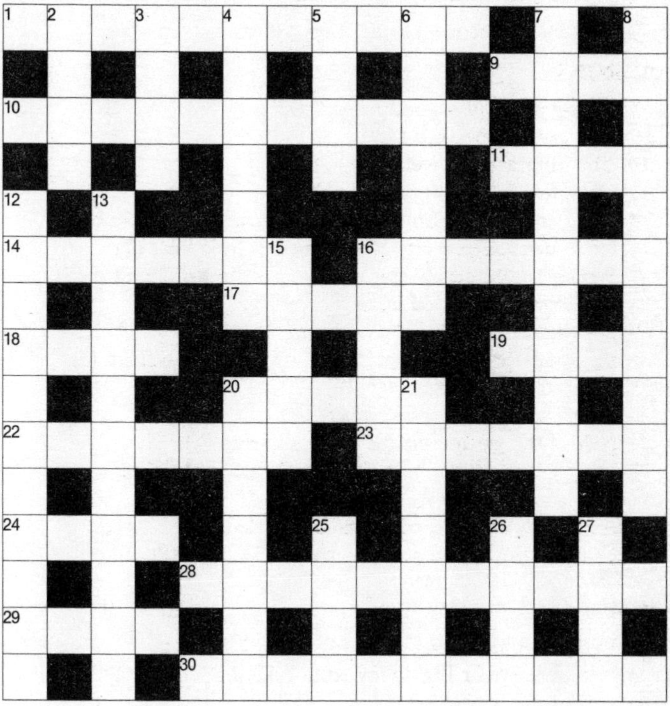

28

ACROSS

7 Small rises that naturally lead to bigger ones? (9)
8 A white mineral container put outside Burlington House (5)
10 Fidgety urge to do more work (8)
11 Interior type of bangle (6)
12 Ned gets involved with a member of the opposite sex (4)
13 A magazine in colour every bit as good as it used to be? (8)
15 Particulars I was severely critical about in retrospect (7)
17 The war made by 19 Down (7)
20 Having the gentleness of Elia's style? (8)
22 A little coal to fire the place, maybe! (4)
25 If I get time, I must go there . . . (6)
26 . . . and he'll be with me! (4,4)
27 Three points to turn round and attack (5)
28 The finale at the Shoemakers' ball? (4,5)

DOWN

1 Two ducks in a plot given another sort of bird! (5)
2 Gave out, needing some rest at Edinburgh (6)
3 A shocking line, this! (4-4)
4 The end of a debate not far outside an ancient city (7)
5 He voraciously reads, disrupting work when there's plenty of trade about (8)
6 What the foot of the Eiffel Tower consists of? (4,5)
9 Spoils seen better through a telescope (4)
14 Making a workable job of a second marriage? (9)
16 Lay waiting to attack changes made round the wilder part of Australia (8)
18 Reels out in determined fashion (8)
19 French gratitude to an early Englishman (7)
21 I ring up an old missionary centre (4)
23 Struggle of a doctor getting into a garment (6)
24 Floral neckwear (5)

29

19 May 1973: Wizzard's 'See My Baby Jive' is
top of the pops

ACROSS

1 The colour I associate with wrong-doing (6)
4 Secretly decide to return after the dance (6)
10 A foot of water in the diocese (7)
11 Saw how the red wine was served? (7)
12 A dram to which the dustman feels he is entitled! (3)
13 It results in a triumph for the best team of course (5)
14 Artificial way of boating (5)
15 A bloomer strongly urged in the interests of preservation? (7,6)
18 Swords can't lie disordered in this royal building (7,6)
23 Day-labourers having second thoughts about 16 Down (5)
25 Stock-taking device that's in a class of its own (5)
26 Right away? (3)
27 Concealed sort of goal for a Spanish notability (7)
28 Stuck on some point (7)
29 Highway robber who was ruthless and sanctimonious in turn (6)
30 Irritable man of intelligence about to take forty winks (6)

DOWN

1 At home doubtless to guard against risk (6)
2 What could follow his idle production is just dandy! (7)
3 Result of overturning, perhaps? (5)
5 It can become grotesque (5)
6 A document that authorizes disregard of propriety (7)
7 Make progress at a very early age (6)
8 Decide to renounce vice and give up roaming? (6,3,4)
9 Where the tiger's satisfaction with the Rigan young lady was shown, apparently (2,3,4,2,2)
16 Vast age that disturbs one . . . (3)
17 . . . with endless ingenuity (3)
19 Correct batting sequence? (2,5)
20 The end of a race past all restoration (4,3)
21 Outcome of aiming high, presumably (6)

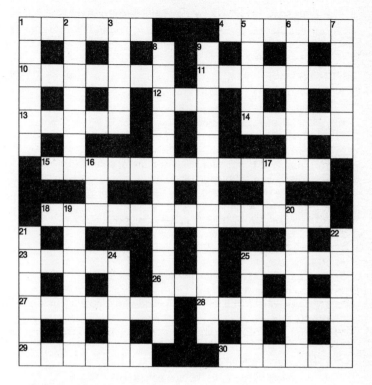

22 Mr Grundy's birthday (6)
24 Obsolete foreign coins I disposed of first (5)
25 A garden spike (5)

30

4 January 1974: The Ulster Unionist Council rejects the Sunningdale Agreement's 'Council of Ireland' proposal

ACROSS

1 & 5 State of the Union? (7,4)
9 A crime against the laws of progress (8,7)
10 Tip for lacquering and polishing, perhaps (4)
11 Burning with enthusiasm, yet not allowed to carry on with the job (5)
12 New World currency used in Europe sometimes (4)
15 Crave to play with little restraint (7)
16 A figure that will gradually disappear when the freeze ends (7)
17 Saw a Blackburn player in the lead (7)
19 Police car taking us the back way round a Berlin prison (7)
21 They cater for thirsts in Nova Scotia (4)
22 He'd put in little work, but didn't despair (5)
23 Battered cars replaced by the RCT (1,1,1,1)
26 Small price to pay for maintaining one's position in society (3,12)
27 Close call when you mustn't miss a trick? (4)
28 A power line that may last for very many years (7)

DOWN

1 A reminder men hold me to (7)
2 One often called upon to sell newspaper information (8,2,4)
3 Climber going round Henry of Navarre's scene of triumph (4)
4 It tends to confuse the man who may bridge the gap (7)
5 Fierce female bringing fuel up over a headland (7)
6 A Scottish division, or what it may march to, perhaps (4)
7 Apparently somebody in no mood to laugh at the first entry in this column (3,4)
8 Put me below with the day-to-day record – they must be gone through anyway (14)
13 Lark or monkey in credit (5)
14 Noisy dispute over an upland tree (5)
17 End weep easily – fabricated show of teardrops (7)
18 Flower of defeat in rabble rising (7)
19 He's read the cut version (7)

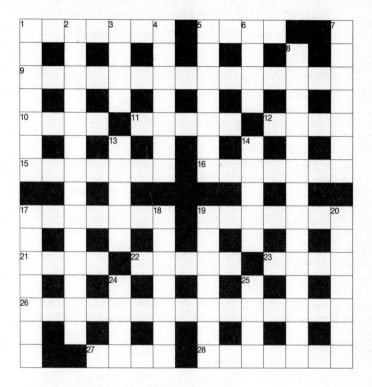

20 Weird epithet for fresh food ? (7)
24 A good shot that has plenty of beef in it! (4)
25 Extra wording put up over an arch, maybe (4)

31

13 September 1975: 'Sailing' by Rod Stewart

tops the charts

ACROSS

1 Its possessor will never be forgotten (11,4)
9 Quick reply I mail in the royal exchange (7)
10 Cocaine preparation coming from the sea (7)
11 Bring pressure to bear on the laundry (4)
12 A basket unable to stand rough treatment? (5)
13 Legal argument is merely a bit of simple arithmetic (4)
16 Spritely explanation for trouble in the air? (7)
17 She requires a change of habitat (7)
18 Rejected birds wryly sad about being taken for granted (7)
21 A London theatre page in a Commonwealth capital (7)
23 A style no longer here? (4)
24 Amid shattered calm I demand what is due (5)
25 Constructive idea (4)
28 State where Ephesians reposed their trust? (7)
29 Lilac initially no good in an Arab republic (7)
30 Lemon-coloured wading bird holding a quill back – a sight not to be missed in Wyoming (11,4)

DOWN

1 All one can get out of industry? (7,8)
2 Travel first in a strange land? (7)
3 A roll of selvage material (4)
4 Retains in the shape of the solid part of the fat (7)
5 Subtle writer of 11 is it? (7)
6 A catch one is delighted to display (4)
7 In a small way it is round a reconstructed tunnel (7)
8 A sign of surprise, maybe (11,4)
14 Its purpose is to secure a pile of potatoes (5)
15 Sailor and Turkish governor brought together in a place of worship (5)
19 Malicious gossip can when boys are turned out (7)
20 Dora's changed about £2 for other currency (7)
21 An excerpt from Ontario's top foreign poet (7)
22 Italian meal for which no plate is changed (7)

Alan Cash

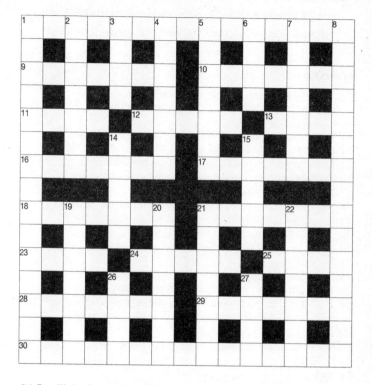

26 It will do for pudding if you turn up the gas ring (4)
27 Deliver it at no cost (4)

32

18 November 1976: Spain's parliament establishes democracy after thirty-seven years of dictatorship

ACROSS

1 The margin within which astronauts are trained to operate (5,5)
9 Constructive idea (4)
10 Unfair conditions (3,7)
11 A clip given a twirl at the top (6)
12 Make a note of deposit (3,4)
15 Evidently hasn't a good word to say for beers brewed outside Great Britain! (7)
16 We'd first see what the cattle did (5)
17 See 3 Down
18 An outer cover supplied within the motor industry (4)
19 'Then turn not pale, beloved ——, but come and join the dance' (Carroll: *Alice in Wonderland*) (5)
21 Elves or fairies that have a heavy duty laid upon them (7)
22 Sort of feminine habit that is highly revealing (7)
24 Row about doctor required to construct a log-cabin (6)
27 The fielder to deal with the matter at issue? (5,5)
28 Unable to move quickly (4)
29 Poet slowly converted to point of most distinct vision (6-4)

DOWN

2 Top-drawer footnote about a fabulous poisoner (4)
3 **& 17 Across** Limerick man who drew extensively on his travels (6,4)
4 Marine fauna of Wales reclassified (3-4)
5 Painful consequence of a spell of hard labour? (4)
6 Irate tip about changing gear (7)
7 Not what the censor uses when he decides to cut a film (5-5)
8 An idle loss dispersed in every direction (2,3,5)
12 Successfully tackles a removal job? (5,2,3)
13 Divine lady to whom Sophocles turned for inspiration (6,4)
14 Vengeful female trio who came from Scandinavia and not Nova Scotia (5)
15 In tranquillity I have another shot at the exam (5)

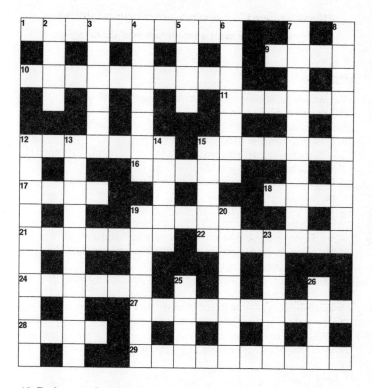

19 Rather too formal a description of a potato diet (7)
20 Bluejackets accommodated in a cool resort in Switzerland (7)
23 In sunny lands they grow oddly solemn (6)
25 Surrey men are at home there (4)
26 Ruin the United Nations likewise supported (4)

33

11 March 1978: Nine Palestinian guerrillas hijack a bus in Tel-Aviv, killing thirty-four civilians

ACROSS

7 Paradoxically, one sometimes has to turn left to take it (5,4)
8 I cast about and had a shot (5)
10 Do nothing but stoke up in a French naval base! (2,2,4)
11 How to solve a cryptic puzzle? (6)
12 A complex knight with no heart (4)
13 What Mrs Mopp has to do to secure wild mustard (8)
15 Valuable feline I enter the Royal Society of Arts to write about (7)
17 Putting on weight (7)
20 The firm's new planning officer? (5,3)
22 I get young Ronald to even things out (4)
25 Odour without old city split by struggle for a Spanish bishopric (6)
26 Got out of an injection? (8)
27 Cold fish (5)
28 It draws people below the streets of London (4,5)

DOWN

1 Roman soldier and what he had to tramp? (5)
2 Bleach when it comes in (6)
3 Fresh drink served hot to clubmen? (5,3)
4 Skill concealed by choice Scottish football team (7)
5 Uninspired writer in a toboggan and unable to move freely (8)
6 A beggar can put in to repair it (9)
9 She's somewhat subdued naturally (4)
14 Elite force trained until they are ready to drop! (3,6)
16 Even a good typist can make no impression with it (5-3)
18 A rest-room in which smoking is prohibited (5-3)
19 Arranging quite an old thing (7)
21 Empty witticism of debatable validity (4)
23 They have news or disseminate it (6)
24 Kind of cartoon in which good man is pursued by disreputable one? (5)

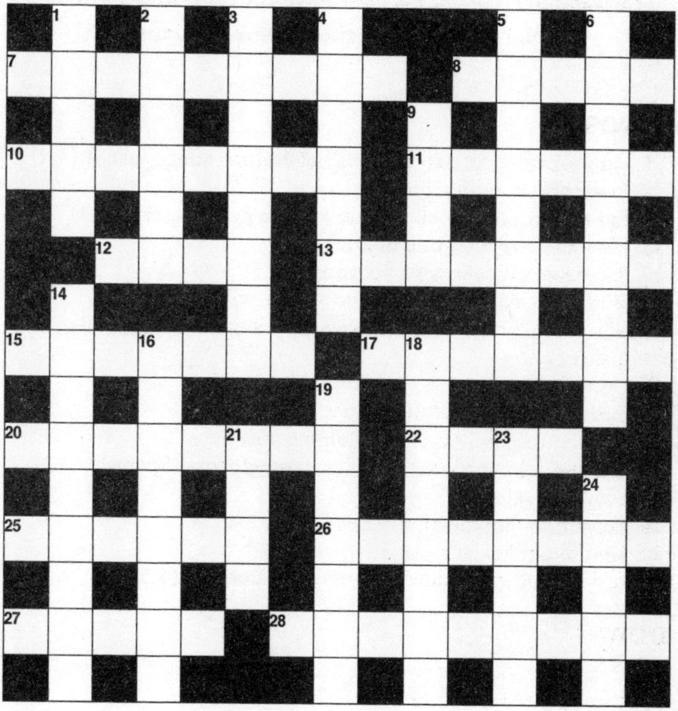
1
2
3
4
5
6
7
8
9
10
11
12
13
14
15
16
17
18
19
20
21
22
23
24
25
26
27
28

34

ACROSS

1 Suitable refreshment for an ultra-Protestant temperance
rally? (9)
9 Ridiculous farce about a bottle of water (6)
10 Arcadian walks for devoted brothers or sisters? (9)
11 A coming event in the church calendar (6)
12 No less sure to find out? (9)
13 Quick-firing weapon brought round to a Frenchman (6)
17 Amusing trifle? (3)
19 Offered to the highest bidder (3,2,2,7)
20 Somewhat unhappy member of the Long Parliament (3)
21 He won dramatic fame in dividing a pasture (6)
25 'Ha-ha,' said the lexicographer, defining this low
bounder! (4,5)
26 Tropical palms that make parrot-cries (6)
27 Sent in a letter of resignation? (9)
28 Not quite the sort of man who is belted in New York! (6)
29 Got a bread order cancelled (9)

DOWN

2 Very much like sauce? (6)
3 Is among those who vote against aural distractions (6)
4 In short, not a West Country domain (6)
5 What the sleepy village became when the city took it
over? (9,6)
6 Ingeniously deceptive use of the pack? (4,5)
7 A marsh plant made of different materials (5-4)
8 Having relevance to the point, can somehow repent
about it (9)
14 Aromatic gum (9)
15 A creature that can fly from the north coast (9)
16 We'll hurry over and get Veronica (9)
17 The spinner heading the averages? (3)
18 May turn up in Polynesian diet (3)
22 Stance of one who is out at elbows (6)

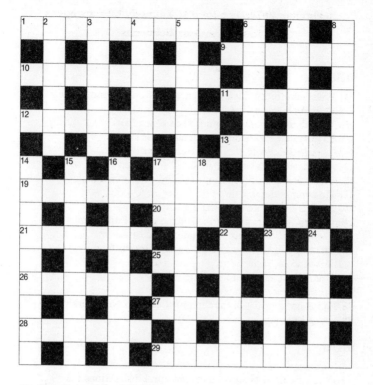

23 The first cabin girl? (6)
24 Agree to give way when confronted with the bill (6)

35

**3 October 1987: Dr John Alderdice is elected leader of
the Alliance Party of Northern Ireland**

ACROSS

1 Still more incapable of feeling what 2 will go into? (4,6)
6 A lively dance to wind up with (4)
9 Their trainees are prepared to take orders (10)
10 It flies about in two different directions (4)
13 I strive frenziedly to make another call (7)
15 Sad reflection about a gate-crasher on view in
theatreland (6)
16 A secret code of little or no importance (6)
17 One of our bigger training centres (4-4,7)
18 Return article with four points to Arctic explorer (6)
20 A record with no accompaniment (6)
21 Blatantly in favour of relative advancement (7)
22 Artist from Somerset typing a letter (4)
25 Someone to inspect a magnificent face-mask (10)
26 In hesitation we get the flagon (4)
27 What the sentry said to the Quaker whose papers were
in order? (4,6)

DOWN

1 A piece of cake from an overseas youth centre (4)
2 'The moan of doves in immemorial ——' (Tennyson) (4)
3 Sent an order to a French seaport (6)
4 They are empowered to act as union negotiators (8-7)
5 A remedy for sickness (6)
7 Worldly people? (10)
8 Independent film trouble-shooter proves long earner (4,6)
11 Heavily punished first offenders (4,3,3)
12 Strings will have to be pulled for it to be effective (10)
13 Chaps who work on rigid lines (7)
14 Enormous disaster – somehow I can't take it in (7)
19 Frenchman leaves whisked albumen to become cloudy (6)
20 Change colour? (6)
23 Man, for instance, seen as a tissue of lies (4)
24 Jejune I am in a way (4)

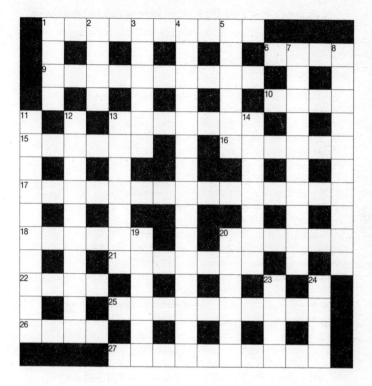

36

ACROSS

1 A charge brought up in the world of commerce (5,4)
8 Just what the doctor ordered! (9,4)
11 Has some meat stewed (4)
12 An imp that is after information (5)
13 Extent of ground gained in the Third Crusade (4)
16 Had turned to rock flowers (7)
17 Going round trying to sell a field sport (7)
18 The converse of countryfolk? (7)
20 Small craftsman's bow tie, maybe (7)
21 Joshua's father's sisters (4)
22 A slur that may have to be examined microscopically (5)
23 Prima donna eager to make a come-back (4)
26 Its members are under orders to keep quiet (6,7)
27 Hunting dogs put outside in wicker baskets (9)

DOWN

2 Short bill brought in about ethnicity (4)
3 Chests for which the Civil Service is about to bid (7)
4 He infiltrates the navy with his doctored foreign wine (7)
5 Not the end of the team (4)
6 The punter will be lucky if he can do it (4,3,6)
7 Laymen who are qualified to hear confessions (13)
9 A memento of one's death, possibly (9)
10 He can't get by without public assistance, poor chap (6-3)
14 Furiously angry quartet breaking cover (5)
15 Mark II? (5)
19 It seems out of place for Jews or Arabs (7)
20 Small body of troops also included in the project (7)
24 The Bear River in America! (4)
25 Go over a series of items (4)

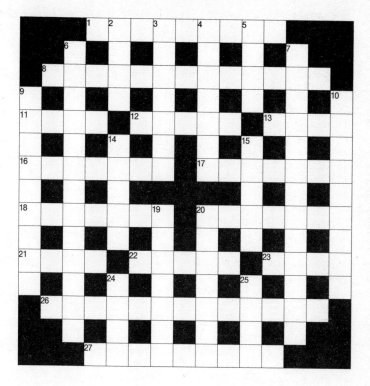

Bert Danher

Bert Danher, crossword compiler extraordinaire, was fond of introducing himself to *Telegraph* readers as 'the man who is Thursday', because he created crosswords for the Thursday edition of the *Daily Telegraph* for almost twenty-five years. But the sobriquet also alludes to *The Man Who Was Thursday*, G. K. Chesterton's novella encompassing anarchy, God, human nature, peace, religion, social order and war, all parcelled together in a satiric commentary that is still relevant today. And Danher's clues were also little gems of commentary. He once said that his inspiration as crossword setter was the 'ah' factor – the clue that, even if you don't solve it, will elicit that exhalation of delight when the solution is revealed. Danher jewels include:

Clue: One raises the issue at tea-time (4,5)
Solution: *High chair*

and:

Clue: Cowardly balloonist (7,2,1,6)
Solution: *Chicken in a basket*

Brilliant!

Bert Danher was a Liverpool man, born in 1926 into a large extended family. The son of a plumber, his time at Liverpool Collegiate was cut short by his father's death – as his cousin put it, 'The thought that staying at school would be a good investment was just not a starter to the world of the workers.' So he left school at fifteen and became a clerk with the Liverpool Cotton Commission. He trained as an RAF aircrew member during the Second World War, but did not see active service, instead being redirected to work as a Bevin Boy. Being a six-foot-four-inch lad in a three-foot-high header at a colliery was not very productive, so he was switched to farm work. After National Service, he became an insurance inspector at Beaumaris in Anglesey for eight years. He managed to teach himself Welsh, joined the Menai Bridge Brass Band, forsook the violin (which had been his father's favoured instrument) for the flugelhorn and discovered cricket.

His first marriage disintegrated and he returned to Liverpool, took up the French horn and became a peripatetic music teacher, occasionally playing with the Royal Liverpool Philharmonic under Sir Charles Groves and later forming the Merseyside Concert Orchestra, an amateur orchestra that gave Sir Simon Rattle one of his first conducting jobs at the age of sixteen.

In his late forties Danher married again, and it was his second wife, Lin, who encouraged him to pursue his ambition to become a crossword compiler. His first puzzle appeared in the *Guardian* in the mid-1970s. Initially his interest in crosswords had been kindled by his Uncle Jim, who had also worked at the Cotton Commission. The *Guardian* was followed by *The Times* and the *Financial Times*, and when the *Telegraph* needed a new crossword compiler in 1978 Bert Danher's work stood head and shoulders above anybody else's.

You could say he had a weakness for anagrams, but in reality it was a strength. He would sit with some Scrabble tiles in front of him and footle around with them until he came up with an anagram of brilliance such as 'talcum powder' from 'World Cup Team'. He had a genius for such apposite anagrams and, indeed, witty clues.

But Danher's greatness as a compiler came from his fascination with the little things of crosswords. He was a man for whom the adage 'practice makes perfect' was a way of life. He practised all the time, and what he practised to perfection was the *Daily Telegraph*'s Quick crossword.

For those readers who are unaware of it, the Quick crossword always has its first and second solutions linked – indeed, sometimes it is the first three or four or five solutions that are linked, but Danher usually confined himself to the first two, and he would connect them into the most delightful puns.

Here are two that were a real joy:

Clue: Dried stalks (5)
Solution: *Straw*

Clue: Kind of hat (5)
Solution: *Beret*
Giving 'straw-beret' or 'strawberry'

Clue: Fairy-like (5)
Solution: *Elfin*
Clue: Ghost (7)
Solution: *Spectre*
Giving 'elfin-spectre' or ''ealth inspector'

And one that is engraved on my memory for life:

Clue: Botanical gardens (3)
Solution: *Kew*
Clue: Animal (5)
Solution: *Brute*

Before I let you have the punch-line, I will confess that when I received the Quick crossword that contained these two clues I paced the *Telegraph* building in Fleet Street murmuring to myself '. . . Kew brute, Kew brute, Kew brute . . .' I could not get that pun! I recall some very odd looks from fellow employees of the newspaper as I traversed the corridors of power muttering away to myself. In the end, in desperation, I phoned Bert Danher and asked him to elucidate. He sounded very bemused. 'It's "Kew brute",' he said. 'Yes,' I replied. 'I know the solution is "Kew brute" but what is "Kew brute"?' Trust me, explaining a pun over the phone is not an easy task. In desperation, Danher said, 'You know, the mathematical thing, three times three times three is three "cubed" and the pun is *cube root*.' Salvation!

I am convinced that the time and trouble that Danher took over these Quick crossword puns formed the *roux* for the brilliant sauces of his cryptic clues. Take his:

> **Clue:** Faint from endless deprivation (3)
> **Solution:** *Wan*

So simple, so elegant, so apposite. Or:

> **Clue:** Toothy Tom from Tarporley, perhaps (8,3)
> **Solution:** *Cheshire Cat*

Charles Dodgson would be proud! Or:

> **Clue:** Butter and milk producer (5-4)
> **Solution:** *Nanny goat*

Perfect!

These clues are Danher at his acme! Clever, fair and oh, so amusing! What more can one ask from a crossword compiler? Well, you can ask him to be a crossword editor. And that is exactly what the bright, shiny new *Independent* did for its launch in 1986. Danher found the job quite taxing. 'It's a lot more complicated than I thought it would be,' he once said to me ruefully. More telling, however, was the dictate that, as crossword editor, he should provide puzzles only for the *Independent*. Danher called a halt to his editing career in 1987 and concentrated on his true love – compiling crosswords for all the heavyweight papers.

Danher was to be the first *Telegraph* crossword compiler to provide puzzles for all the (then) broadsheets, though he was not to be the last. This departure was of great benefit to *Telegraph* crossword solvers – it extended the type of clues they were capable of tackling, gradually stretching them slightly in all directions. Of course, Danher was also the first *Telegraph* crossword compiler to create puzzles in the computer age – that is, at a time when solvers were slowly coming to terms with the advent of the computer society. New words – bits and bytes, ROMs and RAMs – entered the language, and crossword compilers embraced them with glee as another arrow for their quiver of crossword tricks. *Telegraph* solvers, to be honest, were less enthusiastic initially, but over the later decades of the twentieth century learned to accommodate and, indeed, welcome them.

To leave you with the impression that Danher was solely a crossword compiler, albeit a brilliant one, would be unjust. Much of his success as a compiler – as with Barnard and Cash – was the result of his catholic knowledge. He was one of the main setters of questions for *University Challenge* in the days when Bamber Gascoigne was the question master, and, as mentioned earlier, he was a consummate musician who tried whenever practicable to have a musical allusion in his first Across clue. Music ran in that large extended family of his. Danher was introduced to crosswords by his uncle, who also introduced his own son, Paul, to crosswords. Whereas Danher was to shine in the world of crosswords, Paul was to shine in the world of music. According to Danher's widow, Lin, 'Bert used to boast to people about his famous cousin. And cousin Paul [that's Sir Paul McCartney to the rest of us] used to boast about his famous cousin, the crossword compiler.'

But I will leave the last word on Bert Danher to a blogger in South Africa writing in 2002:

> Pray silence for a minute, in memory of an old friend who has died at the age of 75. The strange thing is that I didn't know his name until I read his obituary in the *Weekly Telegraph*; it was Bert Danher, and he was a crossword compiler for many years . . . I have been enjoying [his] gentle little jokes in puzzles for a quarter of a century and wondering who was responsible, because crossword compilers are nearly always anonymous. But now, Bert, I'm finally on to you: plumber's son, collier, insurance inspector, music teacher, and finally crossword compiler so eminent you were asked to produce a special puzzle for no less a fan than Elizabeth the Queen Mother, for her hundredth birthday. Thank you for the fun over the years. I, and thousands like me, will miss you sadly.

'Ah', but the clues live on!

37

ACROSS

1 A striking bar counter! (9)
8 It takes a turn for the better (8,5)
11 Marsh grass seen in Windermere edge (4)
12 Kingdom having the old royal mile (5)
13 You're less of a good-looker with this (4)
16 Big bomb's got name mixed up (7)
17 All debts paid? Have a sun and air passage! (7)
18 Betweenwhiles, man's got to change (7)
20 Possible effect of a canine disturbance (7)
21 Tender, we hear, from a dyke-builder (4)
22 My! About to sin? Excited with drink! (5)
23 Good swimmer looking pale on Sunday (4)
26 Set people moving in the theatre? (5-8)
27 Chains not required for the upright (9)

DOWN

2 Man, for instance, lies about (4)
3 Irishman with bird is a typical example (7)
4 Isle of Wight's goads? (7)
5 Couples opening Somerset House in London (4)
6 Bureau? (7,6)
7 This striker is not back at work (6-7)
9 Instrument with sort of key for the band-leader (4-5)
10 Shut up! step inside – it's deadly! (9)
14 Boards at the Traveller's Rest (5)
15 French aunts were always inclined to lose this feather (5)
19 Corrupt senator's crime (7)
20 Royal Navy one in their spare dress (7)
24 Perhaps Granny is potassium-negative (4)
25 Chap running rings round race (4)

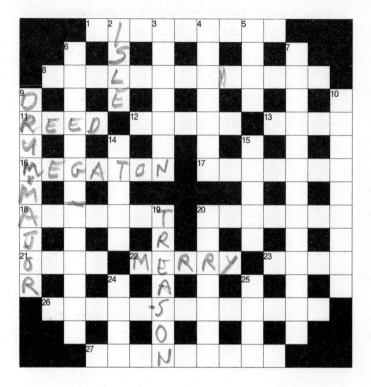

38

5 May 1980: SAS rescue ends Iranian embassy siege

ACROSS

1 Musical figure of integral parts (8)
5 A secondary highway overseas (6)
9 Common cheek to bear this colouring? Only by mistake (8)
10 Gift of old money (6)
12 Burdensome punishment given to named persons only? (4-5)
13 Jack the packman (5)
14 Heavy blow, the square cut (4)
16 Main road (3-4)
19 Church to clean out its eastern section (7)
21 Unaccompanied, walking-on part (4)
24 Girl needing daily refreshment (5)
25 Parson into handyman activities gets Yellow Pages (9)
27 Make angry North agree, somehow (6)
28 Will exercise revolution when sapper leaves and I take over from you, by the sound of it (8)
29 Off-peak calls? (6)
30 Such a beef might employ many vessels (3-5)

DOWN

1 Flowers that split the upper class (6)
2 Breaking camp inside it shows a strong influence (6)
3 Famous school rising over degree (5)
4 That's deficient – boot-polish has no lid (7)
6 Vote against Potter's last object (9)
7 Top gear in Covent Garden? Lummy! (5-3)
8 Acted there within but wavered (8)
11 Range of paranormal psychology (4)
15 Chief spirit in red port (9)
17 Kitchen-vessel seen at Henley at end of July? (8)
18 How Wordsworth became delirious? (8)
20 That's a dicey way of getting home! (4)
21 Cor! Goes like the Dickens – what a character! (7)
22 Like Gray's herd, long overdue (6)
23 Ring, we hear, the young bird (6)
26 Boy displaying scar (5)

Bert Danher

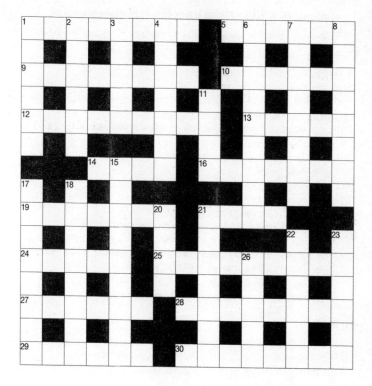

39

6 December 1982: The Irish National Liberation Army
(INLA) explodes a bomb at the Droppin Well bar and disco
in Ballykelly, killing seventeen people

ACROSS

6 Settle area for Kerry show-site perhaps (4,9)

8 Cash advances not suitable for sinking-funds (6)

9 Demurred uncertainly, done in! (8)

10 Mischief-maker of Wimpole Street (3)

11 Admitting poet drops opening lines (6)

12 When tea's served, wrap up (8)

14 Escort vessel to equip with sails – lot on the outside (7)

16 Excuse swindle perpetrated (7)

20 Name of Russian worker in police-station (8)

23 Coe's last circuits need energy – how time can slip away! (6)

24 Old English king too much for Marlowe? (3)

25 Thick slice of bread at end of drive? (8)

26 This used to make a hole in capital assets (6)

27 Man's after rent revision for share-croppers (6-7)

DOWN

1 Taking flight in space perhaps with little gravity . . . (8)

2 . . . gives power to observe from twin orbits (8)

3 Instrument of penetration used in spectrum petrology (7)

4 Extra-large rainbow-god (6)

5 Entertainment of American origin can be anemic (5)

6 Water supply overdrawn – cleverly deduced! (4-6-3)

7 Begonia developed near the SE Alps (9-4)

13 Faint from endless deprivation (3)

15 Champion one for cards (3)

17 e.g. Leonora observable on river . . . (8)

18 . . . I am in to hinder measurement across (8)

19 Break journey, choke not working (4,3)

21 My jostling for example disturbed nudger (6)

22 Wait on part of that tender (6)

Bert Danher

40

3 December 1984: Poison gas leaks from a Union Carbide factory in Bhopal, India, poisoning thousands

ACROSS

8 Gravity attaching to witch-craft in desert (4)
9 Inboard propeller (3)
10 The low tars in them damaged our ratings . . . (1-5)
11 . . . hold the high tar (6)
12 Well off, perhaps in retirement (8)
13 Do Britain's union characters develop such defiance of authority? (15)
15 Breaking the law, you begin to be comfortably off (7)
17 Cheese made unnaturally high? (7)
20 Do rule in the house (5-10)
23 Players' entrance at Wembley? (4,4)
25 The Ag in cloudage? (6)
26 Fighting a lawsuit (6)
27 Foolish sort helping Euclid to build a bridge (3)
28 Parliament to keep fasting (4)

DOWN

1 Grave in Lemnos turned over (6)
2 Flat lock is a frontal feature (4,4)
3 Earthbound? Absolutely (4,2,3,6)
4 Power to live and be at the head (7)
5 Smashing botanist perhaps and believer in the miraculous (15)
6 Rag doll worth, to me, about twopence (6)
7 Shock seeing bats in reverse order (4)
14 Expression of triumphant surprise when I leave mid-western state (3)
16 Letter from Greece airline relies on, in short (3)
18 Pop article in French newspaper (8)
19 Stuff during tea-break (7)
21 Subject for doctorate he sits, possibly (6)
22 French port St Anne converted (6)
24 To edge forward a little at a time is socially acceptable at church (4)

41

30 October 1986: Jeremy Bamber starts life imprisonment for the murder of his parents, sister and twin nephews

ACROSS

1 Toothy Tom from Tarporley, perhaps (8,3)
9 Sweetener given to fortune-teller? (4-5)
10 G-grind clutch (5)
11 Weaver who can move in one direction only? (6)
12 A doctor ordered fresh air, so, and very best food (8)
13 Dulcie bad in geometry (6)
15 No fast food, this! (8)
18 Moon dies away and masks appear (8)
19 Absorbs half day benefits (6)
21 Too little for a lot (8)
23 As apprehensive as a crowned head? (6)
26 Master and king by name (5)
27 Sort of roll, A–F, etc.? (9)
28 Contemplate game of cards on a big scale (11)

DOWN

1 Accomplished, like Lancelot Brown in the garden (7)
2 Striking effect of someone clattering about (5)
3 Iran is hot, but changeable, for a recorder (9)
4 Clothes that are fun for students (4)
5 He throws his objects, involving rats and mice (8)
6 Blake's regular, bright night-burner? (5)
7 Black stuff for nearly all paths, perhaps (7)
8 Needs, we hear, wise man in service (8)
14 Wise or Wisdom? (8)
16 Are those on it calling taxmen 'Sir', perhaps (9)
17 Signs of vitamin deficiency? Try this double Brie-spread (8)
18 Takes twice the time to make old tunic (7)
20 What a heavenly colour! (3-4)
22 Father leaves town near Glasgow for refit (5)
24 Terrier with no drink is taken for a walk (5)
25 Adamson's place at hospital? (4)

135

42

25 June 1987: Catholic civilian shot dead outside his home in Belfast by the UVF

ACROSS

1 Butter and milk producer (5-4)
8 Almost ruing sharpness developed for this garden instrument (7-6)
11 Pledge made in the boathouse (4)
12 Travel leaders take our trip in Cornwall (5)
13 Sell out of retail establishment (4)
16 Satirize the French legislator with nothing on (7)
17 Selector who, presumably, was never in a mendicant order (7)
18 Making a splash, graduate has night out (7)
20 Coarse fabric made from two male animals (7)
21 Principal section of Circle Line here first! (4)
22 Doolally British troops (5)
23 Gets ten letters from school (4)
26 Style following standard decline, without regard for meaning (6-7)
27 Tied, perhaps, after no-ball? Send the offender overseas (9)

DOWN

2 Italian flower a lot of sailors ring (4)
3 This kind of shirt is not for evening (3-4)
4 Georgia's endless ruse concerning stomach (7)
5 Encourage crime in Lincoln Square (4)
6 Summer of American hit, it turns out (13)
7 Staff arrangement as alternative to box-allocation (13)
9 Tender for marine craft (5-4)
10 Isolated fellows start tenanting flat (9)
14 Pick-me-up which often accompanies mother's ruin (5)
15 Low church leaders behave apathetically (5)
19 One who works hard in the orchard (7)
20 Assail doctor in panel (7)
24 Credit letter you wrote to 10 on which the matter turns (4)
25 Bird talk (4)

Bert Danher

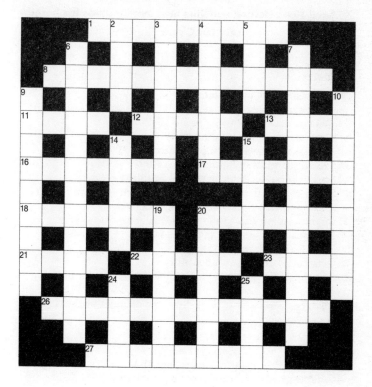

43

27 April 1989: Beijing students take over Tiananmen Square in China

ACROSS

1 Famous seat in Derbyshire (12)
8 Proposition from me to her? (7)
9 Stumps drawn on leaving pitch? (3-4)
11 Referee with work outside is in clover (7)
12 Piece laid down according to Mosaic Law? (7)
13 Dismissed soldiers for deviating from the usual (5)
14 It is held on the range in part of Texas (9)
16 How we looked as gales howled? (9)
19 Piece of rotten cheese or fish (5)
21 French tapestry lo! being woven (7)
23 He speaks his words in play (7)
24 Cancel out fully in explosion (7)
25 Accurate summary to a point (7)
26 Shorter actor can be one who scores (12)

DOWN

1 Mild sort of chap (7)
2 Nobleman, with honour, sometimes accommodates a sleeper (3-4)
3 Photography in which petal semi-opens? (4-5)
4 Engineers able to provide this second repair (5)
5 As a joke, say, a lot of stuff for eating (7)
6 Oil applied to bats, wild in Leeds (7)
7 Brake for Victoria, for example, on coach (7-5)
10 Is one equally successful with ladders? (5-7)
15 But not 26's recording material! (4-5)
17 He can retard a favourite, of course (7)
18 Mean to deal in sea-food, we hear (7)
19 Brown chap touching Circle Line? (7)
20 More dapper French painter (7)
22 Wavering response from English poet (5)

Bert Danher

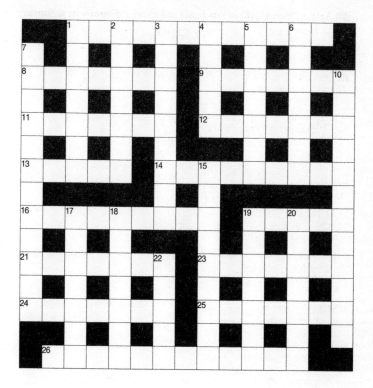

44

19 July 1990: BASF plant in Cincinnati explodes in flames

ACROSS

1 Loaf sliced carelessly in mining areas (10)
6 Record that may slip (4)
10 Reprobate rake, but good at heart (5)
11 Gymnastic feat which could impress the field? (9)
12 Sinister port-worker (4-4)
13 A yarn of two cities, in digest form (5)
15 Apathy is revolutionary in trade expansion (7)
17 Low note heard in oceanic areas . . . (4-3)
19 . . . great volume for transporting people (7)
21 Rhythmic beat when church holds wild dance (7)
22 A French writer has to let jerseys out, we hear (5)
24 Swear at LA litter problem (3-5)
27 Start school? (9)
28 Pretence of outspoken fellows (5)
29 Bordering on being tight-fisted (4)
30 Pieces lent out in epidemic (10)

DOWN

1 It stops in Ireland (4)
2 L-shaped bar reveals ancestor with club (5-4)
3 Winged squadron? (5)
4 Declare former title (7)
5 Scoffed at dried-out editor (7)
7 Euclid's fifth proposition, perfect in conception (5)
8 Can noodles become damaged by these rows of trees? (10)
9 One who has charge of trumpeters, perhaps? (8)
14 Discharge of tar mixture (10)
16 Elegant girl coming out elated (8)
18 Feeling thrill? (9)
20 Arrest for such an attack (7)
21 Pick up is part of the service (7)
23 Food for Dad's Army? (5)
25 Standing a beer is magnificent (5)
26 Make much of garden-party (4)

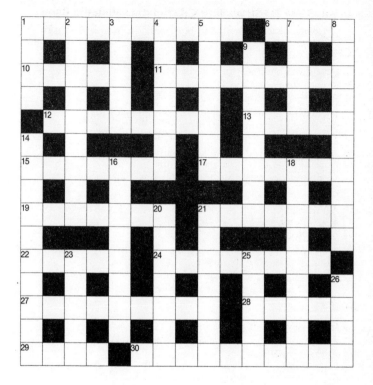

45

14 July 1994: Thirty-fifth International
Mathematical Olympiad is in session in Hong Kong

ACROSS

1 Jet from here still requires a propeller (5-6)
10 Waterlily mean a great deal to America (5)
11 Spectacles needed for this detective with riddle? (9)
12 Where people find flattened rings in cereals? (9)
13 Go out encased in gold for so long (5)
14 Sock of glary design to the English? (6)
16 Common clergyman's worship non-denominational initially (8)
18 Power thing, the atom? (8)
20 Present most excellent ring to woman (6)
23 Ways of one in Staffs, say? (5)
24 Drunken Alec on bar port (9)
26 Method rests with these hospital attendants (9)
27 A wicket almost taken? How alarming! (5)
28 No half-price resort for one who likes the French way of life (11)

DOWN

2 Change in legal terms (5)
3 Conversion of sea-fuel is easy (7)
4 Old Bobby useful in the kitchen? (6)
5 Fixes regular dates? (8)
6 Round university, great trouble and abuse (7)
7 Alice prodigal perhaps in this long cold-spell? (7,6)
8 Patent passenger list (8)
9 Like a really good book, one that cannot be squashed? (13)
15 Fish territories of bays (8)
17 Be Alpine, perhaps, like ordinary people (8)
19 At home, more certain to require an underwriter (7)
21 England's first two trees? Rubbish! (7)
22 Lancashire's weaving centre almost full very quickly (6)
25 King of Mercia left such refuse (5)

Bert Danher

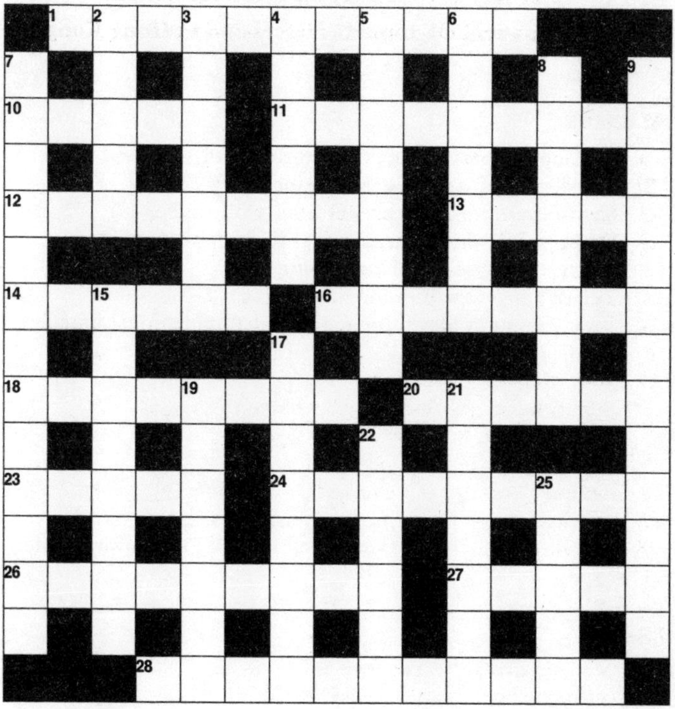

46

**5 November 1998: Myra Hindley loses her second appeal
to overturn her indefinite life sentence**

ACROSS

1 Post-Impressionists affect the value of his collection (11)
9 Gangster placing cowl in front of chimney (7)
10 Song of loyalty from worker at border (6)
12 Hand crack up in coal-mine? (7)
13 National, say, the rate of exchange? (7)
14 Mockery of youth-leader joining club (5)
15 Small restaurant has front facing lake (9)
17 Marble, the most plain, is of poorest quality (9)
20 Hit bottom (5)
22 Lock with loose spring? (7)
24 I, McLeod, out of air (7)
25 One in factory making plastic (6)
26 Stand in Uttoxeter racecourse (7)
27 New perpetrator of off-the-peg clothes in France (4-1-6)

DOWN

2 Break for girl in religious setting (7)
3 Tim liable to break out – that can be checked! (9)
4 Food and drink to someone (5)
5 Post requiring literary knowledge (7)
6 One producing beads for a knitted garment (7)
7 They who take stock from Phil's forest? (11)
8 Spud finds big sum at Job-centre (6)
11 Containers taken from secret places (11)
16 One shows how high a Viscount is (9)
18 Western fisherman and fiddler (7)
19 Rave about high priest having faith (7)
20 Typical orientals, showing little heat (7)
21 Test of gold and lead, possibly (6)
23 Add measure of drink during flight (3,2)

Bert Danher

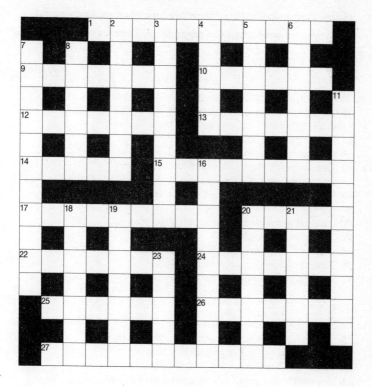

47

ACROSS

1 Years of training to produce cheap pinstripe (14)
10 Works both ways taking valuable fur? That could be challenged! (9)
11 Coppers found in open celebration (5)
12 Concentrated in a stressful situation (7)
13 Cut a way through the wharf to church (6)
15 Music not suitable for lullabies? (4)
17 Deride Dutch house for its flowering shrub (4,6)
18 Do in? (5,5)
20 The main mine opening to find coal stratum . . . (4)
22 . . . new number is lower (6)
23 American whiskey with a chocolate-flavoured biscuit (7)
26 Run in section of race, with courage (5)
27 Severe measures to get rent reduced (9)
28 Guard sauntered aimlessly with students (14)

DOWN

2 Songbird – one under pressure going into mine (5)
3 Revolution becoming apparent (6)
4 No blame now involving duchess (10)
5 American composer taking up one side of old records (4)
6 One who exhausts English politician over row? (7)
7 Ran, inched out in handicap (9)
8 Settling in advance? (14)
9 Yet more devout than five hundred, say, coming from Isaiah? (6-4-4)
14 Flatfish Authority providing fun for kids on the move (10)
16 King or king's jester? (5,4)
19 English clergyman, one who builds churches? (6)
21 Stiffened linen, mainly, for white man in West Indies (6)
24 Alcohol bringing calls of derision, we hear (5)
25 Second vehicle that was once wound? (4)

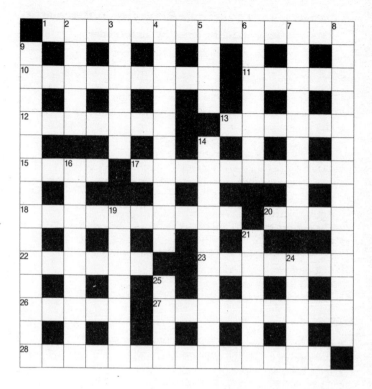

48

6 June 2002: An asteroid explodes over the Mediterranean between Greece and Italy with a force more powerful than the Nagasaki atomic bomb

ACROSS

1 Recent move on board agreed in football club (9,6)
8 Old cold rhubarb (5)
9 Doing away with seaweed, a nostalgic idea in part (8)
11 Wizards cheeky in sex change? (7)
12 Agree to split up (7)
13 Off-peak call? (5)
15 Pit worker can be so scathing (9)
17 Appropriate time for cutting bar prices (5,4)
20 Time short in this world? Here's a word of sympathy (5)
21 Men trod carefully with this ornament in a bar (7)
23 Basil, perhaps, remaining in lead? (7)
25 Self-banking flying machine (8)
26 Usual not to finish Italian opera? (5)
27 Novel with undisclosed plot (3,6,6)

DOWN

1 Bursary, we hear, for Little Jack Horner? (7,5)
2 Wife needs assistance to produce young (5)
3 High tars in a body? (9)
4 Carriage when changing trains on time (7)
5 Warning given when fencing begins (2,5)
6 Nothing heard in prisons (5)
7 Widespread demonstration of public opinion, in the main (5,4)
10 Hibernate far away, this silly person? (12)
14 Going away for a whole new ball-game (9)
16 Rigid state requiring action at a dance (9)
18 Detached portion of rock from Route 51, possibly? (7)
19 Bond has carpet left on board (7)
22 Run off irregularly with sweetheart (5)
24 Having listeners like some serials, say? (5)

Bert Danher

Ruth Crisp

Of the six compilers in this book, Ruth Crisp is the only woman and the most enigmatic. She was born on 1 January 1918 – a date weighty with expectation in a historic year. But it was a Wednesday, and, as the rhyme has it, 'Wednesday's child is full of woe.' And Crisp's life certainly ticked that box. Whereas the other five compilers featured in this book had fascinating lives that enhanced them and their puzzles, Crisp's life has a smack of tragedy that, to my mind, led her to concentrate totally on her puzzles, to the undoubted benefit of both crossword editors and solvers, but not necessarily Crisp herself.

This intense concentration – a life devoted to crosswords one might say – for more than fifty years produced some of the most sublime puzzles ever to appear in the English language. Each clue was honed to perfection by Crisp and slotted neatly into its allotted place in an elegant crossword. Crisp's clues always read like sensible sentences and never straggled inelegantly through complicated definitions. In fact, they were crisp. How very apposite, I hear you cry – Crisp by name and crisp by nature. Ah, well, it's not quite that simple. For Ruth Crisp was not the name she started with, or even married into . . .

Margery Ruth Edwards was born in Linthorpe, Middlesbrough, the elder of the two daughters of a sculptor. Her father, who created many of the war memorials in north-east England, told her stories of the Greek myths and heroes – 'telling, not reading', she would emphasize. They would go on long walks in the country during which he taught her the names of insects, birds and plants. 'He would take me fossil hunting in the Cleveland hills,' she said in an interview just before her retirement. 'I remember the wonder of first breaking into a rock and discovering a perfect ammonite. I could hardly have had a better basis for a crosswording career than all I learned from my father.'

She did well at school, and her father thought she should go to university, but her mother – a forceful figure – believed that it would only 'give her ideas'. So she left school at eighteen and joined the Civil Service as a telegraphist. There was plenty of work during the Second World War, but then she fell in love and the powers that be decreed that married women could not work in the Civil Service, and so her career came to an end.

The marriage did not last long. Her Polish husband died at the age of thirty-two, the delayed result of ill-treatment, starvation and overwork as a POW in a Siberian coal-mine; he, with other survivors, joined the British forces (after a lengthy spell of hospitalization) in 1942. She discovered with considerable shock that, even though the legitimate widow of a naturalized Briton, she was not entitled to a pension for herself or her child.

'Well, in those circumstances I could only mentally roll up my sleeves and get on with it, earn some sort of living from home,' she told me. 'I tried various abysmally paid things – knitting jumpers of my own design for a boutique, making dresses for a factory (12½p each), composing verses (25p each). None of that was going to keep the wolf from the door.' As a young widow with a small child, with none of today's back-up facilities, she was facing destitution.

And then she thought of crosswords. 'Having been a keen solver from my teens, I had come to know what I regarded as a really good crossword, so I started my compiling career aiming for that standard,' she recounted. 'I spent several days polishing up my first crossword, with plenty of radio references, which I sent to the *Radio Times* – only because I noticed there was a different name on their puzzle each week.' It was accepted and more requested. That was in 1954, the same year the *Manchester Guardian* asked her for one puzzle a week. 'So then I was a regular weekly contributor [two guineas] with a set of grids, and I knew I had found my niche.'

The following year the *Birmingham Post* succumbed to her crossword charms, and in that year she landed a very unusual commission. She was the first and only crossword contributor to *Heritage*, a monthly Catholic magazine. On its demise all issues were handsomely leather-bound into a large book which is now housed in the Vatican Library. I don't suppose many crossword compilers have their works housed in the Vatican Library. Life seemed to have moved onto an even keel. She fell in love and got married again in 1958.

The second marriage was a disaster. Her husband, she told me, was both physically and mentally abusive, and she and her children – she had a second son by this marriage – finally fled in fear of their lives. The marriage ended in the mid-1970s, when she was on the verge of bankruptcy. After the divorce, she finally got her home back, but her husband had destroyed all her records, everything: birth certificates, marriage certificates, photographs and all the records of her crosswords. The coming years also saw an estrangement between Crisp and her two sons. There was a rapprochement between her and her younger son in the months before her death in 2007, but the split with the child of her first marriage was irreparable.

I don't think she ever recovered from this series of disasters. She certainly eradicated her previous persona from existence, changing her name by deed poll to Ruth Crisp. The *Guardian* has pseudonyms for all its crossword compilers, and she had chosen *Crispa*, the feminine form of *crispus*, meaning curly-haired, which she was – she subsequently dropped the final *a* for everyday purposes.

Over the next twenty-five years she methodically put her life back together through crosswords, in 1982 becoming a compiler for *The Times*, which also asked her to set the qualifying puzzle for its National Crossword Championships and crosswords for four of the semi-finals for many years. She added the *Sunday Times* to her bag in 1983 and the *Financial Times* and the *Daily Telegraph* in 1985.

I was a trifle disingenuous in writing that 'Danher was to be the first *Telegraph* crossword compiler to provide puzzles for all the (then) broadsheets.' He was indeed the first compiler to *provide* puzzles for the 'Big Five', but it was Ruth Crisp who first had all her puzzles appear in them. The first issue of the *Independent* on 5 November 1986 carried a Ruth Crisp crossword – chosen for the occasion by Bert Danher.

She worked and worked and worked – for most of her compiling life she worked sixteen hours a day, usually starting at around 6 a.m. She built up meticulous records, finally encompassing around a quarter of a million clues – sometimes up to twenty-six clues for one word. She had to work, she said; there was no other means of support, no pension, no insurance. Over the years she gradually earned enough money to buy herself her one luxury – a spacious penthouse flat high above the Thames Estuary in Westcliff-on-Sea.

She occasionally dragged herself away from her grids to walk along the cliff gardens where she lived – a petite, dapper figure tip-tapping along the path.

She was relentless in her pursuit of the perfect crossword. Her clues were magical:

Clue: A know-all, may be hide-bound (13)
Solution: *Encyclopaedia*

Clue: Where one may see wild birds, not big
    game (10)
Solution: *Slimbridge*
*Slim-bridge – not big, i.e. slim, and game of
    bridge (card-game)*

Clue: A number of bonds are for a ten-year
    period (8)
Solution: *Nineties*
*Nine-ties = a number – bonds. A ten-year period
    = the 90s*

'Solvers can be very clever, but you must not be
too clever when creating a clue. The clues must be
deceptively simple. The art, the elegance, is in the simplicity and the precision. It is something akin to poetry.
You must choose exactly the right word. You can learn
to solve but you can't really learn to compile,' she said
in an interview marking her thousandth crossword for
the *Daily Telegraph*. And solvers did have to be pretty
nifty to crack her clues. Her offerings weren't convo-
luted or esoteric; the problem for the solver was that
their very simplicity and elegance made it extremely difficult to get away from the purported sense of the clue
– which, as every solver knows, usually does absolutely
nothing to help solve the clue. Take the last of her clues,
above:

Clue: A number of bonds are for a ten-year
   period' (8)

It is almost impossible to get away from the idea of
banks, financial institutions and so on, as the sentence
just comprises a subject, a verb and an object. Very
tricky for the solver to actually grapple with a cryptic
meaning.

This was Crisp's great strength as a crossword compiler, and she was well aware of it. Woe betide any
crossword editor who changed any of her clues. Of
course, she always *said* the editor had a perfect right
to change her clues for the better, but she had real
difficulty accepting that her clues could be improved.
Most of the time she was correct but, oddly, sometimes her clues had to be ruffled a bit so that *Telegraph*
solvers would have a better run at them. Anything
that she felt belittled her work was jumped on from a
great height. Once, at the last minute, I changed a clue
of hers because the original, 'Maintain America is in
a spot' (7), was, as I recollect, a little sensitive at that
time. I altered it to:

Clue: Maintain you and me are in a spot (7)
Solution: *Sustain*
*Me and you (or America) = us. Inside stain –
   s-us-tain or 'sustain'*

and she wrote:

I must protest about the appalling clue you have
substituted for the one I offered as 1 Down in

today's cryptic crossword. I am really upset that this should be attributable to me – though I should hope solvers familiar with my careful precision in clue-construction will wonder how on earth such a foul-up comes to appear in a puzzle of mine and realise it is not my work.

Firstly, I would never offer anything ungrammatical, and I shudder at the 'you and me are'. Secondly, any clue must be soundly constructed, and it has to be 'us' *is* in a spot, so 'you and me are' is wrong on both counts . . .

. . . please, do not sully the reputation I value like this.

As you can see, she took her role extremely seriously. But unlike other compilers, she never really embraced the computer age and had a faithful amanuensis who would key in her typed work and send off the disc. She continued working into her mid-eighties, but failing strength and crippling arthritis finally ended her compiling days. As she wrote to me:

I always thought I'd feel quite bereft when my crosswording finally came to an end – it has been my life for so long. I must admit, though, the main thing is relief. Compiling has got harder and harder, taken longer and longer, and left me feeling ever more zonked as the years have piled up.

Retiring, however, brought financial hardship. With a tiny income, non-essentials had to be axed, and that included the *Daily Telegraph*. No more crosswords for Crisp to even solve. She died in her beloved penthouse flat at the age of eighty-nine, two and a half years after she had retired. Of all the compilers in this book, she is the one who poured her whole life into compiling, thereby producing quite extraordinarily brilliant clues and puzzles.

I will leave the last word to her:

I seem to have had a one-damned-thing-after-another sort of life, but you just grit your teeth and get on with it, don't you? But I liked crosswords. It was fun, which I suppose is all it was ever meant to be.

49

21 June 1985: Ruth Crisp's first crossword for the *Daily Telegraph*

ACROSS

1 One such as Daphne won't change colour (9)
9 Latin title used only rarely (6)
10 A course favourite, a light-weight (9)
11 Dread being given a casual sort of shirt by mistake (6)
12 Entrap ten wild characters with sorry results (9)
13 A blow or caress (6)
17 She's made a daring start (3)
19 Far from reserved (7)
20 Rush around the house to find the cat (7)
21 A river in the United States, Kentucky (3)
23 Show clearly against entering a German establishment (6)
27 Told the tale about for example being put down (9)
28 A woman will take in an animal that will hurt (6)
29 Dig in soil correctly, showing great respect for it (9)
30 The prohibition is of ancient Greek origin (6)
31 Coppers take the inmate to be the top man (9)

DOWN

2 A churchman who is forever on edge? (6)
3 Deplore appearance of little river bird (6)
4 Old Venetian business centre where oil and tar may be obtained (6)
5 The queen got up like a queen (7)
6 Management course (9)
7 Eminent directors? Right! (9)
8 A fetching breed of dog (9)
14 Diets vary unfortunately when life is hard (9)
15 Sounds like buccaneers (9)
16 Dull church leader prepared for friction (5-4)
17 The mischievous goddess took some food (3)
18 Question as ruler (3)
22 Slim person addressing about fifty? (7)
24 A man will like this area of the Mediterranean (6)
25 Not French but Latin accepted (6)
26 Flag but to continue to write about mid-evening (6)

Ruth Crisp

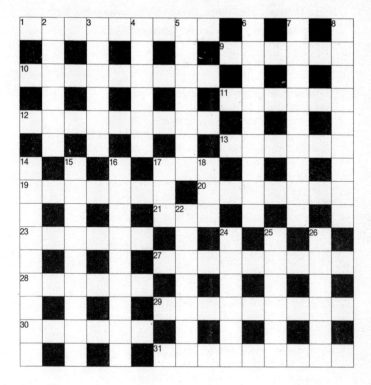

50

**16 October 1987: The great storm wreaks havoc,
killing twenty-two people and felling over 14 million trees**

ACROSS

5 Delayed payment for the entrée (6)
8 Beats using craft about business drive! (8)
9 Badly behaved lads can bring shame (7)
10 Crime committed by a minister losing his head (5)
11 Shocking pastry – throw outside! (9)
13 Unusual palm tree in Wales (8)
14 Schools transport (6)
17 Bow in a church (3)
19 The main part of a ploughman's lunch is cheese and bread (3)
20 Catty, so gets nothing back in remuneration (6)
23 One maybe meant it to be confidential (8)
26 Beat a friend hollow and scoffed (9)
28 No demented itinerant (5)
29 Like corresponding (7)
30 Licensed to make flags (8)
31 Running water is always provided in quarters (6)

DOWN

1 Serial about site of Jericho (6)
2 No one taking part is offensive (7)
3 Coloured person – he was behind William (9)
4 Don't agree to amalgamate again (6)
5 Small bill the clerical assistant should find correct (8)
6 A water-course may upset the French (5)
7 Still only for the male worker around the North (8)
12 Subject to trial experience (3)
15 Good grounds to conserve drink (9)
16 The writer lies about after a fine (8)
18 Control shown as others fall (8)
21 Note it well (3)
22 The vehicle I own is bright red (7)
24 Settled for a good man in distress (6)
25 Most senior set led to effect reform (6)
27 Force a one-penny increase in pay (5)

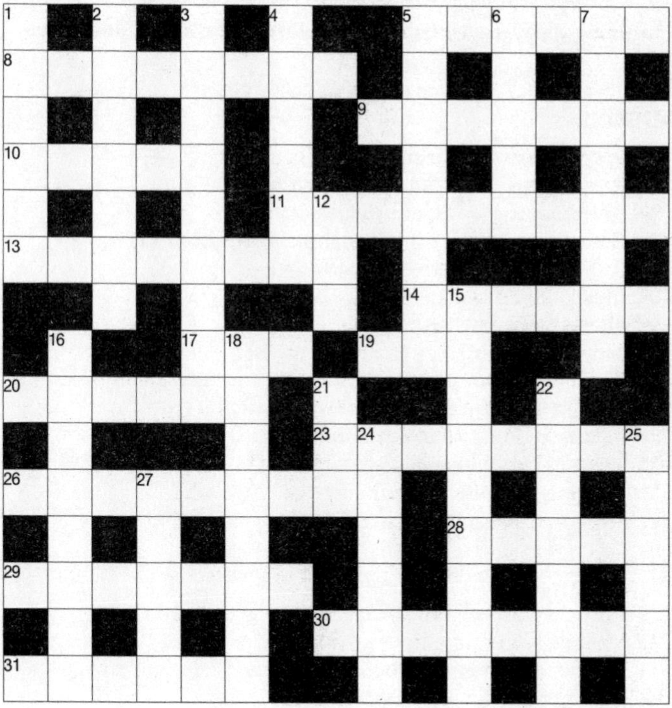

51

25 August 1989: Voyager 2 spacecraft reaches Neptune and sends pictures back to the Earth, 2 billion miles away

ACROSS

1 Precise individual tripping the light fantastic (4,7)
9 It just shows the heights to which one may rise! (9)
10 A woman from a South American country (5)
11 Go astray and there'll be a charge made (6)
12 Colours, with article being read in two ways (8)
13 Mean, which is not in character (6)
15 Turned over only a quarter produced – so perverse (8)
18 Most dice are shaken in the private home (8)
19 Way out English king with English craft (6)
21 A swimmer has to cut back severely (8)
23 Tart as can be making the beds (6)
26 The head of state is a sovereign showing fibre (5)
27 Exciting thing about running water (9)
28 Needing to adapt, but lose more in trying (11)

DOWN

1 Put sow with cow inside and see the growth! (7)
2 She has food in the house – a terrific amount (5)
3 Contributes about a thousand and one according to rules (9)
4 Raising a public school's record (4)
5 Anger – anger about nasty trait (8)
6 Coloured novice (5)
7 Give some pleasure to tot in depression (7)
8 Long retaining a pro to provide personal protection (8)
14 It's unknown for salesmen to be upset (8)
16 Game, though that's of little significance (9)
17 Noted speech (8)
18 Very large and very small figure in small department store (7)
20 Heartless fool with aim to get a decoration (7)
22 Sloth can be the ruination of a musician (5)
24 A friend will offer private backing within a very short time (5)
25 Pilfer a pen? (4)

52

ACROSS

1 Making use of one's time at home (10)
6 Get moving! (4)
10 A point appropriate for the picket (5)
11 People asking questions of pitmen following cut-back (9)
12 The instructor's sister dealt with in writing (8)
13 Stop hundreds with some expertise (5)
15 About to strike, a worker is insistent (7)
17 Area of military activity where the Territorials retreat before regular soldiers (7)
19 Nice tax arrangement – but it's not right (7)
21 Well-qualified man and boy in charge of the stonework (7)
22 Retired doctors exercise here (5)
24 Only a little of any cereal is edible, that's understood (8)
27 Old soldiers set on drill (5-4)
28 Finding limes provided, look pleased (5)
29 Place for a story – not at all vulgar (4)
30 Dogs recovering (10)

DOWN

1 A large number refuse crush (4)
2 Spiritless for a time in an upheaval (9)
3 Round and green and clear (5)
4 Quarter people in rented section (7)
5 Tidy up – start in the passage (7)
7 A topic for discussion in depth: emergent nations (5)
8 Flexibility is shown about one put inside still (10)
9 Don't 21 Down so much when there's no air-current (8)
14 A Westerner losing nothing by chance (10)
16 A swimmer having to carry a weapon is terrible! (8)
18 Exotic Argentine fruit (9)
20 A suggestion offered about royalty's housing (7)
21 Coil – the average German article (7)
23 It is not required to be forbearing (5)
25 Susie's undisciplined children (5)
26 Supports the sovereign for example – the head of state (4)

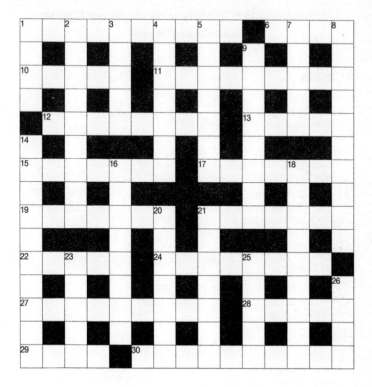

53

**24 December 1993: NASA completes the repair of the
Hubble Space Telescope**

ACROSS

1 The goddess of retribution could make sin seem dreadful (7)
5 Tick is imperative (7)
9 This depends on the listener (7)
10 The woman visited an illicit drinking place (7)
11 Count the money and make cuts (9)
12 Hundreds adapt to it just the same (5)
13 Sovereign power, say (5)
15 A certain European scheme occupying a guy who's loaded (9)
17 The card possibly inscribed by a novice for the church (9)
19 Dressed, though weary (5)
22 A letter some await cheerfully enough (5)
23 Big shot offering dope in French art-gallery (9)
25 Turner, a delinquent pocketing the small change (7)
26 Prevent the top man creating a beastly row (7)
27 Abstracts and deals with the intake (7)
28 A foreign prince making one cross? (7)

DOWN

1 Unnecessarily dispensing with cunning causes exasperation (7)
2 To some degree rave over a beautiful house-plant (7)
3 Smart and virtuous man getting in before midnight (5)
4 The more distinguished person making gestures? (9)
5 A woman getting behind is put out (5)
6 Breaking dates hastily, being really single-minded (9)
7 Encouraged by article, took a chance (7)
8 Traditional oven to include as well as the alternative (7)
14 They're supposed to remember the plane's lay-out (9)
16 Very agreeable associate on a board (9)
17 It's many a girl Edward put in her place! (7)
18 Identifying a winger with a swimmer (7)
20 He faces facts concerning a heel (7)
21 Craft gives the medico some advantage, right? (7)
23 The little page put on airs working in the city (5)
24 A pensioner very often exhibits great courage (5)

Ruth Crisp

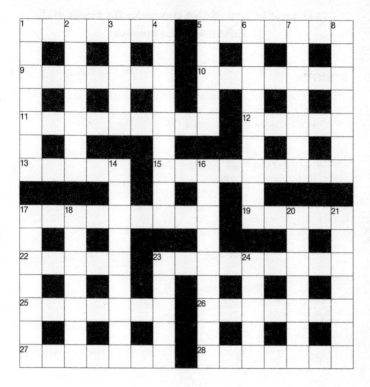

171

54

ACROSS

1 This marine organism has first to be dealt with (8)
5 Reverse? That's in green (6)
9 North-European school-head taken in by a schoolboy (8)
10 Articles about next divine female (6)
12 People getting out – streaming out (9)
13 Cut pieces off a fruit (5)
14 Some appear churlish, some sly (4)
16 Back up in play (7)
19 A discerning gift in a sense (7)
21 Battle involving a hundred soldiers (4)
24 Free entertainment makes the heartless sailor scoff (5)
25 The woman with money avoids wildfowl (9)
27 Give the underworld boss a month and there's consternation! (6)
28 Boring ties – more variety is needed (8)
29 All out to impress (6)
30 A sport left a snappy note (8)

DOWN

1 Good man – regular guy (6)
2 Setting a worker on edge in Northern Ireland (6)
3 Better impose a penalty, right? (5)
4 Firm stem (7)
6 This is not material for a composer, but it is for a writer (9)
7 The man with will-power (8)
8 Take off underwear – put in a carrier (8)
11 A once-revered figure, as is written repeatedly (4)
15 A footballer it's OK to patronize! (5,4)
17 Disturbances causing tears in the main? (8)
18 He rates the fools bearing with an alternative offered (8)
20 Running water can be such a trial! (4)
21 A crime changing a large part of the Western world (7)
22 A sea-monster turning ocean-going craft over (6)
23 An old Jew having a little less energy these days (6)
26 Getting a large number back is dispiriting (5)

Ruth Crisp

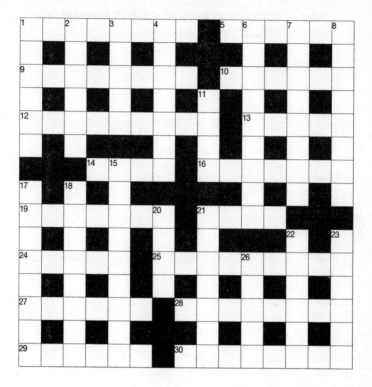

55

**7 February 1997: Fidel Castro says the US should return
huge chunks of Mexican territory it acquired
more than a century ago**

ACROSS

1 Firm taken in by swindles getting the police (10)
9 Page a member about nothing just for show (4)
10 A single male in prison without money – such a drag! (10)
11 It's she composes the dissertation (6)
12 The indifferent dog expert may be set right (7)
15 More inclined to fall in behind (7)
16 Consumer of a tree's produce (5)
17 Right time for agitation (4)
18 Poles turn sanctimonious when a cut's made (4)
19 Interviews about five hundred tip-top players (5)
21 Apt to change round in a game (3-4)
22 Drink a military body finds quite the best (7)
24 Put air in drainage channel ebbing at a rate (6)
27 Fussy detail (10)
28 Yes, a conversion should be simple (4)
29 Doesn't forget to gather in a little reserve (10)

DOWN

2 Electrical units, that's official (4)
3 Breaking down is rare in the mountains (6)
4 Friendly note written in a competent fashion (7)
5 The German lyric gave a false impression (4)
6 Requiring new trestle, he's put in order (7)
7 Principles of study technique (10)
8 An indication of omission upset the poor sap (10)
12 A gamesman familiar with kings and queens (4-6)
13 Conservative outfit get into line (5,5)
14 A stand for peace of mind before cash (5)
15 Divides tips after the year's end (5)
19 Retired person supporting public transport (7)
20 A good time-keeper – in daylight hours (7)
23 Summary about birds to be read up (6)
25 The man engaged in clerical duties (4)
26 A company project (4)

56

ACROSS

7 Ships' rats seem revolting (8)
9 The person who's put in charge (6)
10 Compact made, weapons must be turned over (4)
11 On the watch, with little to pass on (6,4)
12 Directed police offensive (6)
14 Exercise is sound – fall in! (8)
15 Disconcerted indeed when not acknowledged (6)
17 Check on the queen's canopy (6)
20 Game seaman, first-class (4-4)
22 Correct in backing in to get moving (6)
23 Still wanting variety (3,3,4)
24 They'll support certain measures (4)
25 Winger putting money into bag (6)
26 All object about a body of soldiers (8)

DOWN

1 Colours, which is normal (8)
2 Fringe report (4)
3 About mid-December an excellent player appeared (6)
4 People after an apartment find there's competition (4,4)
5 Capital is available for the laundry – to a point (10)
6 A man from Andover none will employ (6)
8 Stay in when broke. That's common sense (6)
13 A rival can not admit being investigated (10)
16 Having eaten, try making an appeal (8)
18 Honours and compliments (8)
19 Fat Greek in need of comfort (6)
21 Modish youth will accept one so decorated (6)
22 Poster ordered with all speed (5)
24 Business is steady (4)

Ruth Crisp

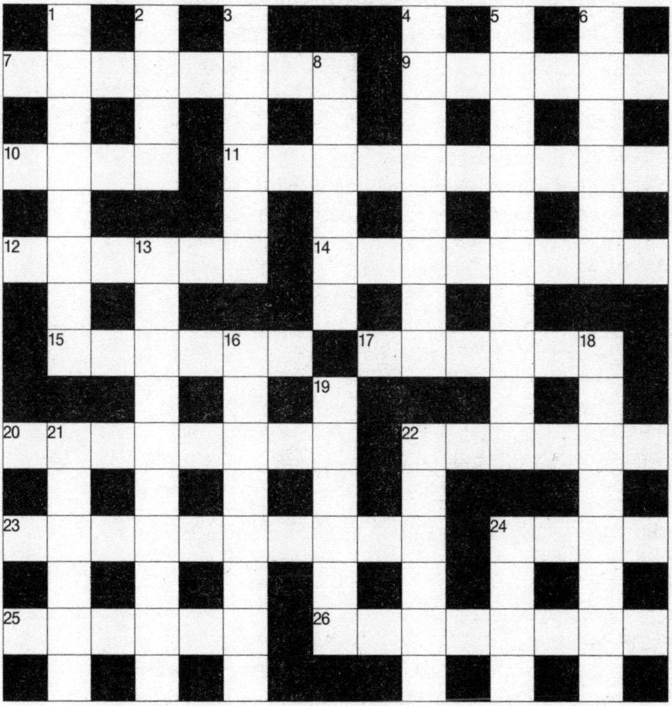

57

16 June 2000: Scientists in Japan build a prototype power unit that runs on natural gas and operates at temperatures much lower than those achieved by many other designs

ACROSS

1 Making a noise and causing annoyance (8)
5 Writing to give tips, maybe about credit (6)
9 Have a late meal with newsmen and check (8)
10 More land – perfect! (6)
12 A lack of good grounding was responsible for this slip (9)
13 Left near-ruined in Northern Ireland (5)
14 A boom? Dispute that (4)
16 Not slow to give voice (7)
19 Being mad at an arrangement that's inflexible (7)
21 Security devices – good buy for retirement (4)
24 Oliver the screw (5)
25 How odd, to prefer a bore! (9)
27 Against beginning concerts traditionally (6)
28 Stick up for people in holiday accommodation (4-4)
29 I object to return of aims to effect reforms (6)
30 Sort of tree to stick in the ground? (8)

DOWN

1 Sound axiom for retaining a good man (6)
2 Recording the head doing an impersonation (6)
3 Yet some think this a peerless ground! (5)
4 Change in rates with more unpleasant outcome (7)
6 Bovine writer's crib? (6,3)
7 Sense hesitation in a foreign dealer (8)
8 Cross right back to the SE state first (8)
11 Some of those remaining will get dry (4)
15 Rendered intoxicated (9)
17 Artistic work it's cheap to reproduce (8)
18 A game girl (8)
20 Drink like a fish (4)
21 Warning must be clear if turning in harbour (7)
22 Delay holding party on a lake in Russia (6)
23 Saw the male sovereign into bed (6)
26 Again and again concerning 'X' (5)

Ruth Crisp

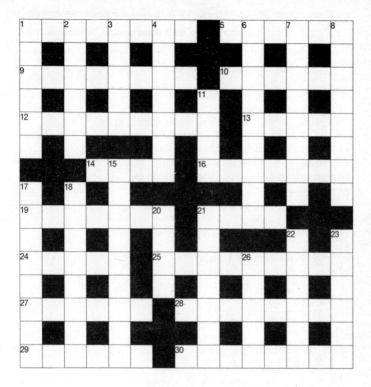

58

27 September 2002: Ruth Crisp's thousandth crossword for
the *Daily Telegraph*

ACROSS

1 A great number will turn awkward and shout (8)
5 Free with money (6)
9 Realizing about fifty may be ill-matched (8)
10 They have a certain partiality for left-overs! (6)
12 See a couple of trainees work, being idle (6)
13 A ball-game – note scores made (8)
15 Railed against but found release in retirement (7)
16 Chance collapse (4)
20 Egghead not backing the public school (4)
21 Placates underworld members (7)
25 *Antigone* translation causing disagreement (8)
26 Property of Oriental, say (6)
28 This is truly nauseating stuff! (6)
29 Contemplate putting alcoholic drink in tea perhaps (8)
30 Bacon could be comparatively audacious (6)
31 A fruit worker given Spartan accommodation (8)

DOWN

1 Set about forming an outfit (6)
2 In fashion for all young people, so it's said (6)
3 Only sherry will be offered in such a ship (8)
4 Joshua's father's sisters (4)
6 A group of managers who have got on? (6)
7 His stock is extremely small – should grow though (8)
8 Trade in film that's improperly distributed (8)
11 Going after an old palace (7)
14 Oils in a compound bond (7)
17 Beasts responsible for the present transport system (8)
18 Study progress, but not in favour of meeting (8)
19 Leaving out nothing on purpose (8)
22 Toil hard, so take rest possibly about four (6)
23 Sending up a chap with a soft hat (6)
24 A woman's time shows on this (6)
27 Inconsistent statement in Pope's document (4)

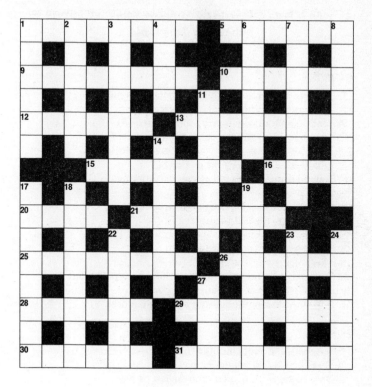

59

ACROSS

1 Place in America that's no longer fashionable? (7)
5 They deal with plants and with clay (7)
9 Note the policeman going around left one a copy (7)
10 The song 'Goodbye to Prison' (7)
11 Done with viewing, which could be a mistake (9)
12 A pert eccentric from the old city (5)
13 A woman is to be put back in charge (5)
15 Chance it maybe – the trainee appears practical (9)
17 Colouring as a result of complaint (9)
19 Cook needs the right sort of oven (5)
22 A seat of learning? (5)
23 The tread's in bad condition – all split (9)
25 He'll enlarge just over five hundred eventually (7)
26 The person showing little appreciation of stylish file (7)
27 Answer for ships' officers in the customary procedure (7)
28 Not permitted to enclose key in short letter (7)

DOWN

1 Reprobate given credit notes with a lot of interest (7)
2 Shanghai, as the reporter might say (7)
3 Detectives go in because they're sour (5)
4 Flighty creature making a poet grin foolishly (6-3)
5 A decoration firm in a hole (5)
6 Can beginner use this kitchen equipment? (3-6)
7 Stretching from the last Ice Age (7)
8 Defence against the main onslaught (3,4)
14 Curses at finding water running over cases (9)
16 People using private transport could be a bloomer (9)
17 A judge of French alcoholic liquor (7)
18 Run laps when out of shape and come to a standstill (5-2)
20 High-flown correspondence (3-4)
21 New diet – it's most well organized (7)
23 Wait to start a game (5)
24 Lit up, being tense (5)

Ruth Crisp

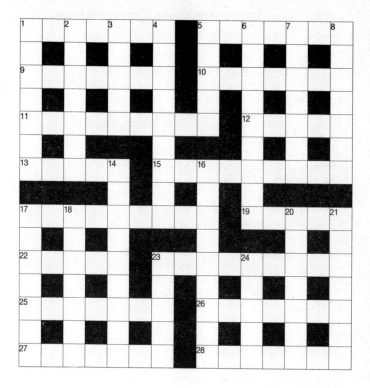

183

60

ACROSS

1 Skilled but unpolished equestrian? (10)
9 In time of war youngsters have to be guarded (4)
10 Meal in part cooked as required by convention (10)
11 Get back, say, into the shower (6)
12 Like the page being seen in jewellery, it's grating (7)
15 Bill of some consequence (7)
16 Note the weakest of the litter appears sound (5)
17 A refusal by a Frenchman (not named) (4)
18 Small creatures turning in the most fearless way (4)
19 Don't sink launch (5)
21 Go on about a race coming to a beastly end (3-4)
22 A pupil left nearer collapse (7)
24 A quarter taken down can be put to rights (6)
27 Dropped new deal in time (10)
28 So with a certain hesitation make a move (4)
29 Viewers should hold on to catch *The Poets* (10)

DOWN

2 Work with aluminium and stone (4)
3 The doctor takes the complete round in a rush (6)
4 Studying for university (7)
5 Stamps and disappears (4)
6 Repudiate touching homily (7)
7 Shabby fellow who'd make a poor player the object of his jibes (10)
8 The person taking charge of one's will (10)
12 Way a speedy individual gets the bird in America (4-6)
13 Grant horse needs exercising, but not over a long distance (5-5)
14 Interrogate cook (5)
15 A woman over fifty making the entry of the year (5)
19 Competency of well-suited head (7)
20 A six-footer engaged in high-rise building (7)
23 Ordering beer at a discount (6)
25 Spirits – and they sound like it (4)
26 Listen to the man with car failing to start! (4)

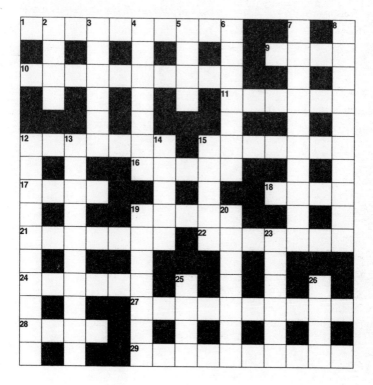

Roger Squires

Leonard Dawe, Douglas Barnard, Alan Cash, Bert Danher, Ruth Crisp – all brilliant compilers, but to the solver's eye each one is more brilliant than the last because each builds on the work of their predecessors.

Dawe started the *Telegraph* crosswords and shaped the patterns and thrust of the clues; Barnard honed the different types of clue – anagrams, cryptics, pushing letters backwards and forwards and inside each other, synonyms, homophones, the use of initial letters – and also introduced sense into the clues; Cash made cross-word clues look as though they had leapt from the pages of a novel; Danher twisted and turned letters into apposite anagrams and witty clues; and finally Crisp refined the process into an art form. And all the while, a special crossword vocabulary was being created:

'flower' – a botanical specimen or a river
    (flow-er)
'issue' – a newspaper, a son/daughter, a topic
'bill' – William, parliamentary paper, account
'worker' – the letters ANT

'a holy man' – the letters ST
'H-O' – H to O – H-2-O – H_2O – water
'drunk', 'organized', 'stew', 'mince' – all
    anagram indicators

And so on, and so on.

And don't forget the sheer number of clues that have been created over the years. The *Daily Telegraph*'s standard cryptic crossword has on average thirty clues and the paper has published more than 25,000 puzzles. That's around 750,000 clues and those are just the ones in the *Telegraph*; add in *The Times*, the *Guardian*, the *Independent* and the *Financial Times* and, of course, all the crossword minnows in the tabloids and you are talking millions of crossword clues, millions of solution words. And there are only around a quarter of a million words in the English language – of course, there are a few thousand phrases as well, but not that many! True, you could emulate Ruth Crisp and have a variety of cryptic clues for each word, but there is still going to be a shortfall.

So what is left for the compiler in the twenty-first century? The personal touch. The final great crossword compiler in our *Display of Lights* is acutely aware that he must imprint his own personal stamp on every clue and crossword.

Roger Squires is a phenomenon in the world of cryptic crosswords. Not only are his puzzles adored by solvers, but if you are solving a crossword in one of the 'Big Five' on a Monday morning, there is a good chance that it will be a Squires crossword. In the twenty years that Squires was compiling crosswords for the *Telegraph* while I was editing them, I can count on the fingers of both hands the number of complaints I have had from solvers about his puzzles. And I suspect that other national newspaper crossword editors would tell the same story. His style of crossword is recognizable – the simple cryptic that appeals to almost all solvers.

Like the other compilers in this book, Roger Squires has had an extraordinary life. Now seventy-six years old, he is featured in the *Guinness Book of Records* as the most prolific crossword compiler. He was born in Tettenhall in 1932 and educated at Wolverhampton Grammar School. In the Second World War, as a deck leader in the Sea Scouts, he acted as a messenger, helped in transferring the D-Day wounded and was a member of a Gang Show entertaining war workers in factories.

From the age of seven, he had always wanted 'to see the world', so, on gaining his School Certificate at fifteen, he joined the Royal Navy as a boy seaman. At twenty, as the youngest-ever seaman petty officer, he moved to the Fleet Air Arm and flew as a lieutenant for eleven years. During the Suez crisis his was the first aircraft to land at El Gamil, Port Said, still under fire, with urgent medical supplies. He joined the Goldfish Club in 1961 by surviving a ditching off Ceylon, escaping from his aircraft when it was sixty feet under water. In fifteen years, Squires visited fifty countries. When not on duty, he organized variety shows, taking them to hospitals in Cape Town, Rio and Singapore. He ran *Ark*

Royal's television station, and represented the Navy at cricket and football, having qualified as an FA coach and referee. He also appeared in night-clubs worldwide under the stage name 'El Squalido'.

In bad weather, when based ashore, aircrew played cards for money, but, as a member of the Magic Circle (yes, he was a magician as well), Squires was barred from doing so, and so began solving crosswords instead. At sea, without newspapers, he started compiling, his first puzzle appearing in the *Radio Times* in 1963. Leaving the Navy that year, he briefly became an entertainments manager at Butlins before turning freelance with magic, acting and crosswords. Television and film appearances included *Crackerjack*, the *Rolf Harris Show* and more than 250 dramas, including *Doctor Who*.

In 1977 his marriage foundered and he gave up 'show business' to look after his two young boys at home. In 1978 he became the *Guinness Book of Records*'s 'World's Most Prolific Compiler', a record he still holds, with over 65,000 published crosswords in 465 different publications, including 58 abroad. In all he holds five *Guinness* records.

He was crossword editor for the *Birmingham Post* from 1981 to 2003, and has regularly compiled for the 'Big Five'. He has had stints on the *Sun*, *Daily Mail*, *Mail on Sunday*, *Sunday Correspondent* and *Observer*, plus more than forty years with the *Evening Standard*. His millionth clue appeared in the *Telegraph* in 1989.

Squires likens his crosswords, now all cryptic, to magic, 'trying to entertain by misdirection'. He avoids obscure words, aiming to provide accurate, good surface-reading clues that occasionally elicit smiles. He is delighted with letters from readers who started solving his puzzles before progressing to more difficult setters.

He particularly likes cryptic definitions:

Clue: Bar of soap (3,6,6)
Solution: *The Rover's Return*

and apposite anagrams:

Clue: All of a tingle, perhaps, from such a beating (12)
Solution: *Flagellation*

He believes his love of words comes from his grand-mother (a Victorian poet) and father, who often won prizes in competitions – asked to sum up 'contentment', his father won a prize with 'wife, whiff and wuff'.

Now remarried, Squires is still compiling. His puzzles distil the essence of the best in crosswords – simple and elegant clues that entertain the solver. They are eminently suited to the twenty-first century, grazing over a wide selection of topics from academia to pop culture – he was the first to find a clue for *Glasnost* and to spot the anagram 'Presbyterians/Britney Spears'.

Roger Squires carries the torch for the contemporary cryptic crossword. He is the latest in a long and illustrious line of *Telegraph* crossword compilers who have entertained – and driven to distraction – hundreds of thousands, if not millions, of the paper's readers in the last eighty-plus years. I wonder who he will pass the torch on to . . .

61

**3 November 1992: Bill Clinton becomes the forty-second
president of the USA**

ACROSS

1 Something we all have in common (6,8)
9 Labels for matches (7)
10 Rent row causes a storm (7)
11 Possibly felt it's not right (4)
12 Dostoievsky's partner in crime (10)
14 A panel on an aircraft (6)
15 Crimes put one's life in jeopardy (8)
17 Bet a long leaping stride is natural to it (8)
18 Slightly deflects the ball and scores (6)
21 Better order meal before I make speech (10)
22 Site in India, grave of Shah Jahan's wife (4)
24 State capital of natal at variance (7)
25 Swallow one drink (7)
26 Chatter-box? (9,6)

DOWN

1 Two girls, one on each knee (7)
2 To have to run away from the police is an unexpected
  occurrence (4,4,3,4)
3 I make an offer in place of a previous quotation (4)
4 Neglect Dad's drink (4,2)
5 Got into a bed made incorrectly (8)
6 Like an astronaut returning – or failing to get lift-off? (5-5)
7 Go under an assumed name (6,9)
8 Sure to change one's ways (6)
13 Genius that outshines all others (10)
16 Near the avenue (8)
17 Where the Ark went fast (6)
19 Not well away from land (7)
20 Saint gets response in church from organ (6)
23 Journey in South Africa (4)

62

4 May 1994: Israeli prime minister Yitzhak Rabin and PLO leader Yasser Arafat sign a peace accord granting the Palestinians self-rule in the Gaza Strip and Jericho

ACROSS

1 Ship in a bottle made by a craftsman? (5-6)
8 Irrelevant description of a ship by the headland (3,3,5)
11 Over the side (4)
12 Drive away from Soho (4)
13 Possibly solve it in bed? (7)
15 Ruth and I are upset about politician making a success (7)
16 Not quite enough to make the GI drunk (5)
17 Sweet kind of music (4)
18 A duck-egg blue (4)
19 Girl gets headstart, having unusual zeal (5)
21 It's largely untrue (7)
22 Suitable dance for the Hunt Ball? (7)
23 Lingering desire (4)
26 Untidy place to note as an eyesore (4)
27 A capital music centre (3,3,5)
28 Game for some drunken flirting? (11)

DOWN

2 Raise 51 feet (4)
3 The estate agent's lying (7)
4 See the Indian creep softly away (4)
5 Do a couple separate in such a serial? (3-4)
6 A misshapen nose ages (4)
7 Everybody is in good health – or expressing discontent! (3,4,4)
8 Is worthless as a cash customer? (2,2,7)
9 They're underage and won't win the vote (3,8)
10 Strictly it's where's the rent due (2,3,6)
14 Pitch is rising first in instrument (5)
15 He's taken to be a criminal (5)
19 Father met in New Delhi air terminal (7)
20 Rock singer (7)
24 Musical Joe's seen twice (4)
25 Unique feature of the common lynx (4)
26 Look for the bishop's office over the weekend (4)

63

**5 August 1996: Atlanta still suffering from the bombing
at the summer Olympics**

ACROSS

1 It measures two attributes of a gymnast (6,7)
10 Available to customers, or about to arrive (2,5)
11 Offensive rumour about a retired doctor (7)
12 Falsified one's accounts? (4)
13 Highlight of 70s fashion trousers? (5)
14 When bulbs come to life? (4)
17 Keeps going, or waits (5,2)
18 Once in the theatre, he demands his money's-worth (7)
19 Reserve player gets no score – with very chilly result (7)
22 N. America's largest meat producer (7)
24 One king is showing the flag 4)
25 Start to speak out as an orator? (5)
26 Become engaged in some sharp practice (4)
29 Comes to school and listens (7)
30 One of the toasts that may be offered with a meal (7)
31 Resolute drama students are (8,2,3)

DOWN

2 Bill goes to the North gate (7)
3 Might be in or even out (4)
4 Aviation spirit (7)
5 Trainee goes round Grand National course (7)
6 An entrance I'd turn in at (4)
7 One may peg out playing it (7)
8 Site for an open-air theatre? (5,8)
9 Stake all on success when there's little choice at the butcher's?
(4,2,7)
15 The remains of a sporting trophy (5)
16 Port and orange (5)
20 Swell watering place (7)
21 One who is against work has a problem (7)
22 Made a come-back after hitting bottom (7)
23 Cast pie out, though it's germ-free (7)
27 Bargain for crop (4)
28 Such a fuss getting to the party (2-2)

Roger Squires

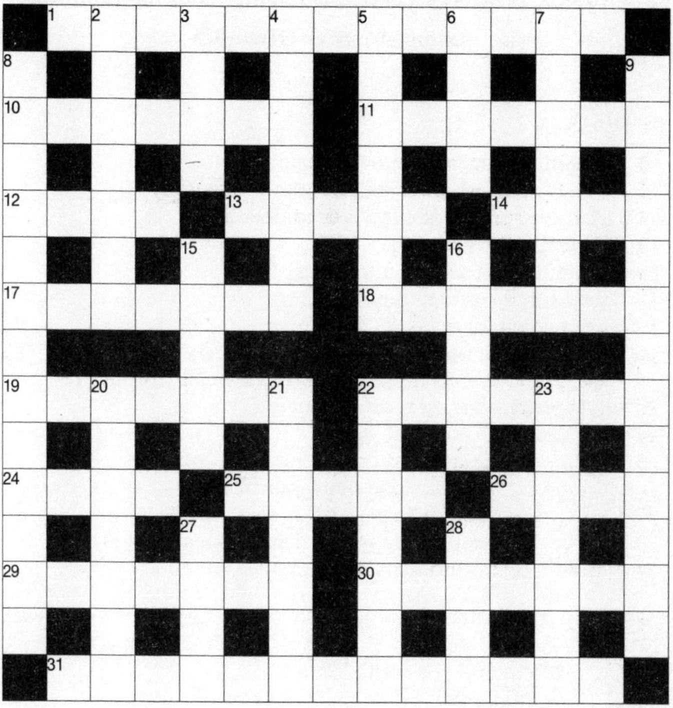

64

**20 July 1998: Two hundred aid workers leave Afghanistan
on orders of the Taliban**

ACROSS

6 Circumvents current faults (5,8)
8 Mother's returning on a vessel – an oriental boat (6)
9 Law agency involved in plot about the Queen (8)
10 One form of eternity (3)
11 I breathe fresh air in part of Spain and Portugal (6)
12 Denounce former husband who may create trouble (8)
14 High and mighty (7)
16 Running easily for victory in the return game (7)
20 Censorious to a dangerous degree? (8)
23 Most diffident about thesis (6)
24 Dismissed when on strike (3)
25 They're important to one's standing as a rider (8)
26 Made a resounding comeback (6)
27 Reforming the unit, remembers repayment (13)

DOWN

1 For an NCO such punishment may well involve stripes (8)
2 Stage one, perhaps, in the development of civilization (5,3)
3 He hopes to find you well (7)
4 Cut down on chesty complications (6)
5 Glass-paper? (6)
6 He takes a stand on a particular case, so to speak (7,6)
7 Concise description of most liqueurs (5,3,5)
13 What you may say when you get the bill? (3)
15 Some intuitive New Zealand bird (3)
17 Wireless user gets a new set in ship (8)
18 Hesitated in speech, being handicapped (8)
19 End of clues or anagram (7)
21 It's so lethargic – prod it to move (6)
22 Crikey, Bunter left hardly any! (6)

Roger Squires

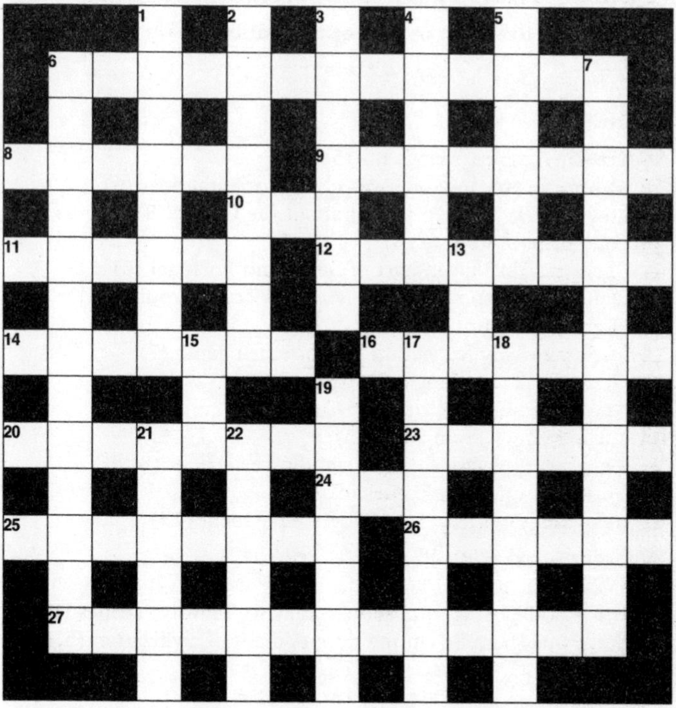

65

3 January 2000: Russia's acting president, Vladimir Putin, steps up the Army's assault on the rebellious republic of Chechnya

ACROSS

1 Frolicking with South African clique? (8)
9 Life after death? (8)
10 Photograph without warning (4)
11 An overdrawn account (12)
13 It can make a man hate what is repellent to him (8)
15 They may be square or round? (6)
16 Advanced one good reason for sacrifice (4)
17 One French port is a key to the others (5)
18 Resistance units serving the Queen (4)
20 Teach fishes swimming (6)
21 Cleaning down (8)
23 Nonconformist who may be best in prayer? (12)
26 Well-produced paintings? (4)
27 Fish cooked as diners required (8)
28 The difference between imports and exports (5,3)

DOWN

2 Tell everyone girl's gained weight (8)
3 Great follower of Dickens (12)
4 Packed as a precaution? (2,4)
5 Going to drop one clanger (4)
6 Minimal sign of intelligence (8)
7 Thanks go to the team transport (4)
8 They often use clubs and bars, but should be fit (8)
12 Tender given backing by Charles Dickens (3-5,4)
14 Completed a meal – while flying? (3,2)
16 Final appointment before military retirement? (4,4)
17 Two students put inside, paying for playground tyranny (7)
19 Unusual gloom in a remote part of Asia (8)
22 Some variation in game line-up (6)
24 Big lake rising in southern Ireland (4)
25 Formerly in older style (4)

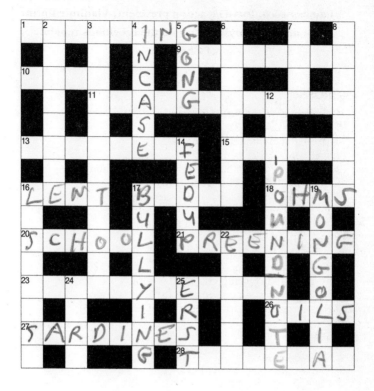

SE
FISH   GYMNISTS

REDUP

66

29 October 2001: Quietest night in Kabul since the American bombardment of Afghanistan began on 7 October

ACROSS

1 Occasion some face with resolution (3,5,3)
9 Burn the fish (4)
10 Tied sort of worker? (5-6)
11 Figure it must be a dud coin (4)
14 I call round on pressing business (7)
16 Man of affairs (3,4)
17 It is in fact a long claw (5)
18 Hundreds pocketed by accountants, the rotters! (4)
19 Sort of oil lamp needs trimming (4)
20 Allude to a palindrome (5)
22 Yet such timber may have been stripped (7)
23 King and two biblical characters free of duty (7)
24 A slap on the wrist (4)
28 Descriptive of a sophisticated traveller? (7-4)
29 A singular occasion (4)
30 The favourite in form (8,3)

DOWN

2 A reflection of what one says (4)
3 It has never been observed in society etiquette (4)
4 Tale a hundred tell (7)
5 The only fish in the sea? (4)
6 And the sailor is first on leave (7)
7 Struggles to maintain faith in the past (3,8)
8 Figure it isn't right when so called (5,6)
12 His patients may be spellbound (5-6)
13 All right in part (4,7)
15 The game's up! Edward's confined to school (5)
16 First of the drinkers finished the port (5)
20 A symbol of house wines (3,4)
21 Firm purpose to settle (7)
25 Smart boy, a lace maker (4)
26 Wise old birds, but slow in development (4)
27 Is the French one ringed in the main? (4)

67

**1 April 2002: The Netherlands becomes the first country
to legalize euthanasia**

ACROSS

1 Sack fathead in anger (5)
4 Relaxed, with lowered pulse (8)
8 Refinements of elegant neckwear (8)
9 Joined in, without being searched (8)
11 Increase general disorder (7)
13 Extremely wicked but safe in our disguise (9)
15 Place to make one's name as a contractor (2,3,6,4)
18 Small gear-case on a bicycle (6-3)
21 Carried on in the nude, perhaps, though embarrassed (7)
22 Record turn-over? (4-4)
24 Instrument used by one making an entry (8)
25 Take an attitude over something that's beneath you (8)
26 Birds of prey often highly-strung (5)

DOWN

1 Present yourself in Gallic style for the meeting (10)
2 Cosmetic surgery fact file distributed (4-4)
3 Points to small boy put in the high chair (8)
4 Record is within a couple of figures (4)
5 Figure it might be an anaesthetic (6)
6 Still rings up, nevertheless (4,2)
7 Bound to have reached the same result (4)
10 Where prompt action is requested (3-5)
12 Crooked men about to plot in an underground vault (8)
14 Hold hands? (10)
16 Lifeless Rugby player at an impasse (8)
17 Enjoying surplus wealth (2,6)
19 Motoring club? (6)
20 The boy found embracing the girl is beaten (6)
22 Fruit for reducing figures (4)
23 The language of Somerset (4)

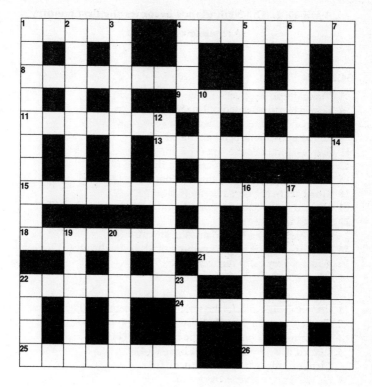

68

17 March 2003: Robin Cook resigns in protest over the war in Iraq

ACROSS

1 Human resource target for Women's Lib (8)
6 Mary's husband makes joke about European Parliament (6)
9 There's something precious in one set of twins (6)
10 Guard sent to breached line (8)
11 Top shelf may be the place for titillating entertainment (5,3)
12 Girl in row is not so scruffy (6)
13 Ideal sales talk of appeal to music lovers (7,5)
16 Listed building visited by tourists in Italy (7,5)
19 Say what you like, it's free! (6)
21 Disturbances dealt with in courts (8)
23 Short odds? That's not fair (3,2,3)
24 Flowers one gets out of bed (6)
25 A man's calling for Australian port (6)
26 Involved in a trying delay (2,6)

DOWN

2 Gaoled drunken ancient (3-3)
3 Piano melodies – duets (5)
4 Cracking assistant for a huntsman (7-2)
5 Favour shown to the electorate (7)
6 Girl making article in stone (5)
7 It takes its turn between washing and ironing (4-5)
8 Claim money round about end of August (8)
13 Detective of more colourful fashion (9)
14 Old-fashioned news broadcaster (4,5)
15 Not only don't come, but prevent others coming (4,4)
17 It sinks beneath the waves (7)
18 The nun wanders around the diocese without being observed (6)
20 It's played in America when one is out of form (5)
22 I had become attached to the Isle of Man in a manner of speaking (5)

Roger Squires

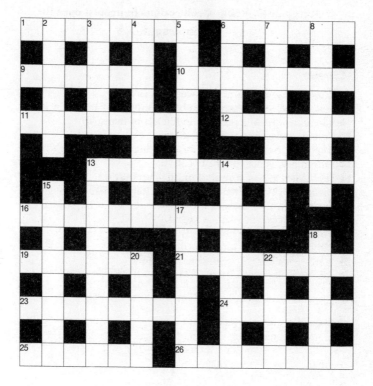

69

ACROSS

1 Anguish descriptive of Scrooge losing a pound (6)
4 Make a tidy packet before Christmas (4-4)
9 Fool to put back a party during Noel, perhaps (6)
10 It's suspended just before Christmas (8)
12 A type of wine (4)
13 Automatic right to go on a toboggan (5)
14 Dry sherry with half a muffin, nothing more (4)
17 Naturally, they add colour to the decorations (5,7)
20 Something afoot in pantomime (5,7)
23 Prompt action to get some of our geese fattened (4)
24 Fancy nothing on the Christmas tree perhaps (5)
25 Fixes the drinks (4)
28 What Cinderella became after twelve (8)
29 On average, a child is someone who is busy at Christmas (6)
30 Time for a mass celebration at Christmas (8)
31 China's unusual paper Christmas decorations (6)

DOWN

1 Unusual harmony about the start of Christmas in the kingdom (8)
2 Winter dancing party? No, but it's thrown for fun (8)
3 Normal procedure exercised by Wenceslas (4)
5 Now it's where the thought counts! (2,3,7)
6 Gather it's what children like to eat at parties (4)
7 Fruit for the Christmas cake is planted in wet weather (6)
8 Glutton takes a long time to finish off the bird (6)
11 Royal address at Christmas (6,6)
15 Time for some juicy clementines (5)
16 Second mince pie a shade of brown (5)
18 Social winter activity after high jinks (5-3)
19 Puts on shows, packed at Christmas (8)
21 Client has no hesitation in this business (6)
22 There's no disputing it was a Scrooge speciality (6)
26 The gift bearers show some imagination (4)
27 Party is a hit (4)

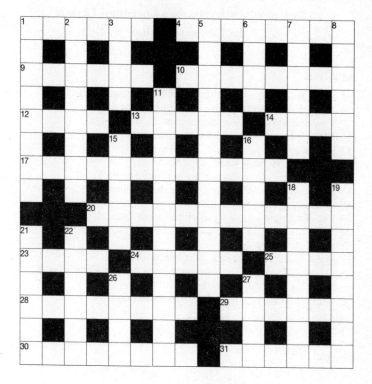

70

ACROSS

1 Christmas package is in the right place for sorting (6)
4 Present comes from French leader in foreign parts (8)
9 Producing endless fruit for Christmas cakes (6)
10 Fifty in carol involving Christmas bells, perhaps (8)
12 It weakens the spirit when party's held back (4)
13 Prepares gifts and cards (5)
14 Bet it's neat rum! (4)
17 Opening words of a favourite carol from her list of ten (3,5,4)
20 Members of the services at Christmas (12)
23 The bird is full of thiamine (4)
24 Number of fingers (5)
25 What about the end of a white Christmas? (4)
28 Like a gaudily wrapped present? Small child hides disappointment (8)
29 It may be worn for the party (6)
30 Swapping presents – the impudence! (8)
31 Vera is seen out at university party (4,2)

DOWN

1 Mistletoe, for example, needs trim as it comes in (8)
2 Christmas present drawer (8)
3 Frosty return for the Arab prince (4)
5 Urge to open an original Christmas gift (12)
6 Mince pie, cold, is impressive (4)
7 A geographical description of Christmas (6)
8 Look for a goose (6)
11 Party refreshments provided by wise man going round America with a car (7,5)
15 He plays a simple part in pantomime (5)
16 Kind of ribbon used for decorations (5)
18 Part of the turkey pulled apart, with luck (8)
19 A blooming avalanche in winter (8)
21 Suggest a present for a child? Excellent! (3-3)

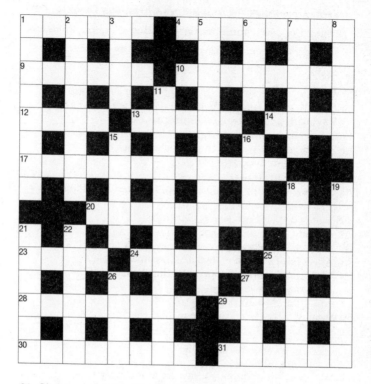

22 Christmas meal inside the German hostelry (6)
26 He turns up for Christmas (4)
27 Nuts – crack almonds to start with (4)

71

4 September 2006: Steve Irwin, the Australian film and TV personality, environmentalist and animal rights advocate, dies after being stung in the chest by a stingray

ACROSS

1 They're soon led astray and may end up in the soup (7)
5 Obliteration is certain after time (7)
9 A spice having no end of use in savouries (5)
10 Such a discussion gives opportunity for falling out (4-5)
11 The crack of dawn? (5,2,3)
12 Quiet argument on the ship (4)
14 Newly nationalized water company may carry this out (12)
18 These workers' benders are excellent! (3,4,5)
21 Mole has snack on river (4)
22 Guess the meaning of this word (10)
25 Everyone bound to be properly organized (3,4,2)
26 A trio involved with proportional representation (5)
27 Nero sprawled on his couch in a toga? (7)
28 Gets inside information in return for savings (4,3)

DOWN

1 Awful barney not far away (6)
2 Bird circles over its quarry (6)
3 Canal employee identified by hair and ring (4-6)
4 Set up works of deception (5)
5 Part of the plans for promotion (9)
6 Jack and Edward retired (4)
7 Support in setting up dinner (8)
8 Willing to finish in debt (8)
13 Old soldiers who got the hump (5-5)
15 Went without saying (9)
16 Interruption at work means reduction in pay (8)
17 One who wallows in merry-making? (8)
19 Take stock of others (6)
20 Take quite a time to enjoy membership (6)
23 Where to find father in the beginning of the year (5)
24 Dance circle lost member (4)

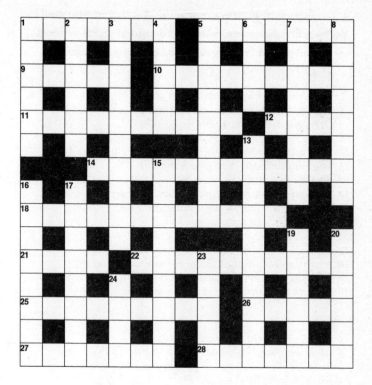

72

ACROSS

1 Humiliate a cricket side on purpose (6)
4 He wrote notes for butcher's order (8)
9 Open out a French bap (6)
10 Finish at a pinch (5,3)
12 First mate right as always (4)
13 Foreign article contains inaccuracy (5)
14 Each one a fairy! (4)
17 Common drinking companions (3,3,6)
20 Notices new sign in a store (12)
23 Perhaps every term holds a recess (4)
24 Ox and cox (5)
25 Measure two notes (4)
28 Put order into project (8)
29 A West African state that encircles a West African state (6)
30 They could be used to make get-aways (8)
31 Run out of clothes (6)

DOWN

1 Clue one composed about power and riches (8)
2 Always in favour of having strong fortifications (3,5)
3 Duck seen on English river (4)
5 They follow the game (12)
6 Union leaders firm – that's great for the Scots (4)
7 Made a run to clinch the match (6)
8 Lunch for a pet at home (6)
11 Festival in various lands – Italy's a possibility (3,6,3)
15 Main meal without a starter? It won't please this man (5)
16 New arrival, we hear, at the docks (5)
18 Permit – strange to relate (8)
19 Writer's star sign (8)
21 The wrong path, say, may hold up the bowler (6)
22 Provide company car (6)
26 Second rank or front? (4)
27 A bit of leave (4)

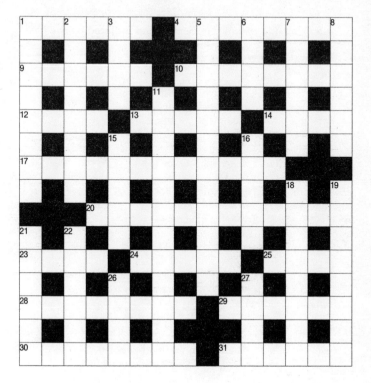

SOLUTIONS

1

ACROSS
- 1 Byron
- 5 Poe
- 8 X-rays
- 13 Raid
- 14 Drake
- 16 Arum
- 17 Aloe
- 18 Raker
- 19 Pile
- 20 Nets
- 21 OM
- 22 So
- 23 Tael
- 25 Swim
- 28 Lop
- 30 Balm
- 34 Spot
- 35 Romeo
- 37 Soit
- 39 Oar
- 40 Corunna
- 41 Inn
- 42 List
- 44 Bilge
- 45 Bret
- 46 Neat
- 47 Sue
- 48 Beer
- 53 Agag
- 57 OC
- 59 ie
- 60 Acre
- 63 Mace
- 64 Crete
- 66 Plan
- 67 Etna
- 68 Harem
- 69 Sort
- 70 Seers
- 71 Gem
- 72 Medes

DOWN
- 1 Brand
- 2 Yale
- 3 Riot
- 4 Odes
- 5 Pram
- 6 Oak
- 7 Ekes
- 9 Rapt
- 10 Aria
- 11 Yule
- 12 Smelt
- 14 Drop
- 15 Eros
- 24 Romulus
- 25 Spain
- 26 Worse
- 27 It
- 28 Loris
- 29 Penge
- 31 As
- 32 Loire
- 33 Miner
- 34 Sol
- 35 Rob
- 36 One
- 38 TNT
- 43 Ta
- 45 Be
- 49 James
- 50 Hoch
- 51 Deem
- 52 Dents
- 54 Gate
- 55 Acne
- 56 Gear
- 58 Crag
- 59 Item
- 60 Apse
- 61 Clod
- 62 Rare
- 65 Ere

2

ACROSS
- 1 Doctors
- 4 Tongues
- 8 Sleep
- 10 Renew
- 12 Tell
- 13 Latin
- 15 Yell
- 16 Nap
- 17 Seem
- 19 Agree
- 21 Idle
- 22 Soon
- 24 Many
- 26 Tots
- 27 Bite
- 29 Sthi
- 31 Term
- 34 Echo
- 35 Calf's
- 38 Toes
- 39 Sou
- 40 Ears
- 42 Chest
- 44 Temp
- 45 Decay
- 46 Sorry
- 47 Needles
- 48 Arsenic

DOWN
- 1 Dentist
- 2 Tall
- 3 Reel
- 5 Open
- 6 Grey
- 7 Skilled
- 8 Sloes
- 9 Pang
- 10 Ripe
- 11 Weedy
- 14 Tart
- 18 Motto
- 19 Antic
- 20 Emits
- 21 Inert
- 23 Ooh
- 25 Ate
- 28 Médecin
- 29 Sherd
- 30 Aloe
- 32 Money
- 33 Aseptic
- 36 Ashy
- 37 Fuss
- 41 Send
- 42 Case
- 43 Tour
- 44 Tree

3

ACROSS

1 Competition
8 Desperado
10 Alph
12 Esau
14 Andes
17 Adorn
19 Viand
20 Air race
21 Tweak
22 Islam
23 Erosion
24 Oxted
25 Stain
26 Skunk
29 Herd
31 Skua
32 Inelegant
33 Delegations

DOWN

2 Oudh
3 Pasha
4 Tweed
5 Traps
6 Oboe
7 Catastrophe
9 Fundamental
11 Protector
13 Small talk
15 Norfolk
16 Elation
18 Naked
19 Veins
26 Scene
27 Ukema
28 Khaki
30 Dime
31 Stun

4

ACROSS

1 Outstanding
8 Plum
  pudding
11 Awry
12 Erin
13 Sidearm
15 Bolivia
16 Yearn
17 Game
18 Odin
19 Papaw
21 Renewal
22 Mirages
23 Lint
26 Bene
27 Tooth
  powder
28 Territorial

DOWN

2 Ugly
3 Summary
4 Alum
5 Dudgeon
6 None
7 Sausage roll
8 Predominant
9 Gravedigger
10 Untarnished
14 Medal
15 Bream
19 Painter
20 Widower
24 Tome
25 Spot
26 Beta

5

ACROSS

1 Broomstick
8 Iota
10 Admiration
11 Pine
12 Dump
15 Respite
18 Crime
19 Ladle
20 Vague
21 Laird
22 Verge
23 Inlet
24 Twain
25 Tweed
26 Granite
30 Reef
33 Eton
34 Reapproach
35 Hale
36 Demolition

DOWN

2 Ride
3 Olive
4 Scamp
5 Idiot
6 Kind
7 Stem
9 Speculator
10 Annihilate
13 Underneath
14 Pretending
15 Reading
16 Ingot
17 Elevate
20 Villa
27 Realm
28 Nepal
29 Trout
31 Esau
32 Fred
33 Echo

6

ACROSS

5 Almost
8 Call to arms
9 Tallow
10 Under cover
11 Animal
12 Incendiary
17 Sly
18 Altar
20 Draw
22 Very
23 Trent
24 Era
26 Still water
30 Cattle
31 Legitimate
32 Office
33 Concordant
34 Slight

DOWN

1 Cannon
2 Sleeve
3 Forced
4 Trivial
5 Astray
6 Multiple
7 Stowaway
13 Core
14 Newt
15 Islet
16 Rydal
18 Avow
19 Trot
20 Dreadful
21 Anything
25 Ringing
26 Select
27 Lotion
28 Armada
29 Extent

7

ACROSS

1 Eighty
4 Obliging
9 Timbre
10 Carousel
12 Metre
13 Aggregate
15 Nib
16 Trout
17 Riddle
22 Creche
24 Bluff
27 Pas
28 Orange tip
31 Caste
32 Trimming
33 Dug-out
34 Right arm
35 Heated

DOWN

1 Estimate
2 Gumption
3 Tormentor
5 Bhang
6 In one
7 Inspan
8 Galley
11 Fabric
14 Rid
18 Dieppe
19 Lobscouse
20 Cut short
21 Affected
23 Eve
25 Porter
26 Fading
29 Gamut
30 Tenor

8

ACROSS

1 Up to the mark
9 Essen
10 Melancholia
11 Trigo
12 Cedar
15 Wells
17 Ale
18 Muse
19 Synod
22 Pedal
23 In use
24 Ypres
26 Sees
27 The
28 Navvy
30 Style
33 Tempo
35 Thereabouts
36 Ounce
37 Done to a turn

DOWN

2 Place
3 Omaha
4 Hock
5 Moose
6 Keats
7 Assiduously
8 Incoherence
12 Composition
13 Daydreaming
14 Rally
15 Weser
16 Leo
20 Nasty
21 Dives
25 PLA
28 Noted
29 Verge
31 Trout
32 Later
34 Dago

9

ACROSS

1 Solitary
5 Hazard
9 Satirist
10 Lessee
11 Mulberry
12 Morris
14 Vivandière
18 Goalkeeper
22 Offing
23 Steerage
24 To obey
25 Obliging
26 Creepy
27 Sennight

DOWN

1 Sesame
2 Lately
3 Turner
4 Restrained
6 Adenoids
7 Assorted
8 Deemster
13 Lamentable
15 Agnostic
16 Calf love
17 Skin deep
19 Benign
20 Paling
21 Weight

10

ACROSS

1 Long Island
8 Idle
10 Democratic
11 Ruin
12 Edge
15 New York
18 Alice
19 Erect
20 Breve
21 Ingot
22 Poser
23 Union
24 Green
25 Usher
26 Earnest
30 Pelt
33 Pro
34 Watertight
35 Kiwi
36 Garden gate

DOWN

2 Omen
3 Glove
4 Surly
5 Actor
6 Dice
7 Flag
9 Breaking up
10 Diving bell
13 Dress shirt
14 Enterprise
15 Neptune
16 Ocean
17 Keep out
20 Briar
27 Aster
28 Norse
29 Sling
31 Evil
32 Twig
33 Phut

11

ACROSS

1 Highlands
6 Porch
9 Vibration
10 Loyal
11 Sweetmeat
14 Below
15 Pyre
16 Wombat
19 Agent
20 Chaotic
22 Ingot
23 Thaler
24 Undo
26 Shiva
27 Asthmatic
32 Alibi
33 Pneumonia
34 Enrol
35 Resistant

DOWN

1 Hives
2 Gable
3 Least
4 Noise
5 Sanity
6 Palm Beach
7 Royal seal
8 Holy water
12 Moth
13 Apropos
16 Whipsnade
17 Magnifier
18 Actuarial
21 Itch
25 Damper
28 Thews
29 Mumps
30 Tonga
31 Craft

12

ACROSS

1, 18 & 33
  Daily Telegraph's
  Ten Thousandth
  Crossword Puzzle
8 Train travel
10 Elia
11 Wits
13 ARA
16 Sharpen
17 Mislead
18 See 1 Across
22 Roguery
24 Nonplus
25 Mug
27 Pupa
31 Seal
32 Evening hour
33 See 1 Across

DOWN

1 Disease
2 Lira
3 Trip
4 Later
5 Goad
6 Anew
7 Seaside
8 Tirade
9 Line
12 Spotted
13 Antonym
14 Amusing
15 Asinine
19 Talker
20 Cryptic
21 Isolate
23 Gape
26 Ulnar
28 Avis
29 Know
30 Shop
31 Suez

13

ACROSS

1 Dachshund
8 The devil to pay
11 Omen
12 Unbar
13 Duma
16 Enchant
17 Dilemma
18 Airless
20 Frailty
21 Idea
22 Fewer
23 Wadi
26 Seventh heaven
27 Afternoon

DOWN

2 Aide
3 Have-not
4 Holland
5 Noon
6 Three-cornered
7 Vacuum cleaner
9 Pomerania
10 Paralysis
14 Haven
15 Float
19 Spectre
20 Freshen
24 Serf
25 Cato

14

ACROSS

1 Marigold
5 Agenda
9 Backward
10 Device
12 Longshore
14 Avast
15 Sad
16 Cement
19 Incur
22 Usual
23 Curare
25 Ado
28 Human
29 Rook-rifle
32 Obtain
33 Head gear
34 Miller
35 Narrator

DOWN

1 Mobile
2 Recent
3 Gowns
4 Largo
6 Grenadier
7 Nuisance
8 Aperture
11 Tester
13 Ham
17 Eglantine
18 Encore
20 Mushroom
21 Gunmetal
24 Ark
26 Effect
27 Nearer
30 Omega
31 Radar

15

ACROSS

1 Merchant
5 Butter
9 Call-note
10 Scales
11 Wardrobe
12 Amused
14 Electorate
18 Convention
22 Unison
23 Flounder
24 Abadan
25 Bedstead
26 Eleven
27 Amenable

DOWN

1 Macaws
2 Rulers
3 Hungry
4 Notability
6 Uncommon
7 Talisman
8 Residues
13 School term
15 Accurate
16 Envisage
17 Desolate
19 Hudson
20 Adverb
21 Bridge

16

ACROSS

8 Virtuoso
9 Not bad
10 Rod
11 Bearskin
12 Ermine
13 In the first place
15 Stand-in
18 Dead Sea
21 Barber of Seville
24 Reveal
25 Betel nut
26 Tee
27 Banana
28 Aperture

DOWN

1 Pigeon
2 Starch
3 Rock of Gibraltar
4 Corners
5 Under the
   weather
6 Stumbled
7 Barnacle
14 Tea
16 Trade gap
17 Nobleman
19 Sol
20 Offbeat
22 Inlets
23 Louvre

17

ACROSS

1 Puffer
4 Marble
10 Tontine
11 Honesty
12 Exit
13 Start
14 Solo
17 White elephant
18 Round of drinks
23 Lots
24 Award
25 Blue
28 Gambler
29 Incline
30 Tenace
31 Ledger

DOWN

1 Patter
2 Finnish
3 Evil
5 Aunt
6 Bassoon
7 Etymon
8 Centre forward
9 Charles Darwin
15 Stone
16 Chain
19 Ottoman
20 Killing
21 Slight
22 Meteor
26 Alec
27 Acre

18

ACROSS

1 Important
8 Generalissimo
11 Emus
12 Booth
13 Blot
16 Amnesty
17 Ratchet
18 Imagine
20 Pabulum
21 Etch
22 Brute
23 Sign
26 Leave the stage
27 Crack shot

DOWN

2 Mien
3 Oratory
4 Twister
5 Nose
6 Return matches
7 Small holdings
9 Negatives
10 Statement
14 Astir
15 Stubs
19 Erratic
20 Putters
24 Aver
25 Otto

19

ACROSS

1 Corkscrew
9 Abutter
10 Beaters
11 Thalers
12 Light soil
14 Merry men
15 Seance
17 Address
20 Asgard
23 Undertow
25 Pneumonia
26 Treacle
27 Ransoms
28 Observe
29 Deferring

DOWN

2 One-time
3 Kitchen
4 Caressed
5 Wattle
6 Put across
7 Streams
8 Presented
13 Imbrown
15 Situation
16 Capricorn
18 Saturate
19 Adverse
21 Grouser
22 Railman
24 Opened

20

ACROSS

1 History
5 Lily
9 Nautical compass
10 Oops
11 Anent
12 Acre
15 Tippled
16 Clinker
17 Call out
19 Crawler
21 Oath
22 Often
23 Snap
26 Slow boat to China
27 Flay
28 Renegue

DOWN

1 Hand out
2 Slum population
3 Omit
4 Yearned
5 Laconic
6 Lamb
7 Pasteur
8 Pancake landing
13 Allow
14 Midas
17 Crossed
18 Tiffany
19 Chester
20 Replace
24 Abel
25 Scan

21

ACROSS

1 Manslaughter
9 Ongoing
10 Test Act
11 Peer
12 Minim
13 Star
16 Isolate
17 Decorum
18 Excused
21 Dilemma
23 Tyre
24 Serge
25 Esau
28 Ray guns
29 Epitome
30 Incandescent

DOWN

1 Magneto
2 Naif
3 Lignite
4 Untried
5 Host
6 Exactor
7 Complimentary
8 Stern measures
14 Manse
15 Scale
19 Carry on
20 Dressed
21 Digress
22 Miss out
26 Tuna
27 File

22

ACROSS

1 Spectacles
9 Flea
10 Husbandman
11 Grease
12 Grieved
15 Hearsay
16 Solos
17 Acne
18 Nova
19 Beard
21 Obvious
22 Delayed
24 Hit out
27 Electorate
28 Nook
29 Deportment

DOWN

2 Plug
3 Cobble
4 Aunties
5 Limp
6 Singles
7 Clear-story
8 Made by hand
12 Gramophone
13 Innovation
14 Doges
15 Hoard
19 Butt end
20 Debater
23 Antrim
25 Peep
26 Eton

23

ACROSS

1 Pharmacopoeia
10 Old hand
11 Forbore
12 Idol
13 Crack
14 Halo
17 Get down
18 Redhead
19 Impeach
22 Wassail
24 Earn
25 Smelt
26 Aery
29 No trace
30 Contour
31 Incense burner

DOWN

2 Hide-out
3 Ream
4 Andiron
5 Officer
6 Ours
7 Isolate
8 Homing pigeons
9 Record players
15 Moral
16 Adust
20 Puritan
21 Hampers
22 Wolf-cub
23 Acetone
27 Game
28 Oner

24

ACROSS

1 Put off
4 A good way
9 Lie low
10 Comedian
12 Butt
13 Fresh
14 Fete
17 Current issue
20 Pitch and toss
23 Arid
24 Mid on
25 Bema
28 Good nick
29 Decays
30 Prompter
31 Broken

DOWN

1 Pull back
2 The stars
3 Flog
5 Grouse season
6 Oyez
7 Waiver
8 Yonder
11 Arctic circle
15 Get it
16 Ruddy
18 Come back
19 Assassin
21 Hang up
22 Kimono
26 Snip
27 Gear

ACROSS
1 Orchestras
9 Coco
10 Percentage
11 Nimrod
12 Greylag
15 Restore
16 Giver
17 Espy
18 Plea
19 Burns
21 Agonies
22 Strewed
24 Immune
27 Fictitious
28 Rani
29 Temptation

DOWN
2 Reel
3 Hockey
4 Sand-bag
5 Ream
6 Spender
7 Court of law
8 Good reward
12 Grenadiers
13 Employment
14 Gibus
15 Reins
19 Benefit
20 Statist
23 Enlist
25 Scum
26 Juno

ACROSS
1 Dockets
5 Beam
9 Vulnerable point
10 Rout
11 Annex
12 Idle
15 Everton
16 Starved
17 Cellist
19 Cantrip
21 Bogy
22 Splay
23 Make
26 National Theatre
27 Rely
28 Chaired

DOWN
1 Diverse
2 Coloured lights
3 Ewer
4 Shannon
5 Billets
6 Alps
7 Pithead
8 Mind over matter
13 Stair
14 Saint
17 Cabinet
18 Toplady
19 Chaotic
20 Pretend
24 Dove
25 Leda

ACROSS
1 Wooden spoon
9 Hull
10 Leave-taking
11 Once
14 Animals
16 Lucknow
17 Ethos
18 NATO
19 Abel
20 Bands
22 Hurry up
23 Stature
24 Lawn
28 First eleven
29 Noes
30 Third person

DOWN
2 Over
3 Dive
4 Notable
5 Pike
6 Omnibus
7 Running Blue
8 Sleep-walker
12 Saint Helena
13 Bitter-sweet
15 Strap
16 Lords
20 Bullish
21 Stoke up
25 User
26 Near
27 Zero

28

ACROSS

7 Foothills
8 Borax
10 Restless
11 Anklet
12 Edna
13 Restored
15 Details
17 Crimean
20 Lamblike
22 Sack
25 Prison
26 Cell mate
27 Onset
28 Last dance

DOWN

1 Booed
2 Stated
3 Live-rail
4 Closure
5 Bookworm
6 Base metal
9 Mars
14 Repairing
16 Ambushed
18 Resolute
19 Mercian
21 Iona
23 Combat
24 Stock

29

ACROSS

1 Indigo
4 Ballot
10 Spondee
11 Noticed
12 Tot
13 Relay
14 Canal
15 Pressed flower
18 Windsor Castle
23 Peons
25 Lasso
26 Off
27 Hidalgo
28 Impaled
29 Turpin
30 Snappy

DOWN

1 Insure
2 Doodler
3 Giddy
5 Antic
6 Licence
7 Toddle
8 Settle for good
9 On the face of it
16 Eon
17 Wit
19 In order
20 Last lap
21 Upshot
22 Monday
24 Soldi
25 Lupin

30

ACROSS

1 & 5 Married life
9 Motoring offence
10 Nail
11 Fired
12 Peso
15 Overact
16 Snowman
17 Proverb
19 Spandau
21 Inns
22 Hoped
23 RASC
26 Low subscription
27 Slam
28 Dynasty

DOWN

1 Memento
2 Retailer of news
3 Ivry
4 Dentist
5 Lioness
6 Fife
7 One down
8 Intermediaries
13 Caper
14 Rowan
17 Paisley
18 Blossom
19 Sheared
20 Uncanny
24 Bull
25 Span

31

ACROSS

1 Everlasting fame
9 Riposte
10 Oceanic
11 Iron
12 Frail
13 Plea
16 Gremlin
17 Tabitha
18 Assumed
21 Adelphi
23 Away
24 Claim
25 Plan
28 Indiana
29 Syringa
30 Yellowstone Park

DOWN

1 Earning capacity
2 Explore
3 List
4 Stearin
5 Ironist
6 Glee
7 Annulet
8 Exclamation mark
14 Clamp
15 Abbey
19 Scandal
20 Dollars
21 Ariosto
22 Polenta
26 Sago
27 Free

32

ACROSS

1 Outer space
9 Plan
10 Bad weather
11 Apical
12 Put down
15 Rebukes
16 Lowed
17 See 3 Down
18 Rind
19 Snail
21 Spirits
22 Topless
24 Timber
27 Cover point
28 Fast
29 Yellow-spot

DOWN

2 Upas
3 & 17 **Across**
  Edward Lear
4 Sea-fowl
5 Ache
6 Enraged
7 Flick-knife
8 On all sides
12 Pulls it off
13 Tragic muse
14 Norns
15 Resit
19 Starchy
20 Locarno
23 Lemons
25 Oval
26 Undo

33

ACROSS

7 Right road
8 Shied
10 Be at rest
11 Decode
12 Knot
13 Charlock
15 Persian
17 Loading
20 Ideas man
22 Iron
25 Oviedo
26 Immunity
27 Bleak
28 Tube train

DOWN

1 Miles
2 Whiten
3 Green tea
4 Partick
5 Shackled
6 Mendicant
9 Edna
14 Red Devils
16 Space-bar
18 Opium den
19 Antique
21 Moot
23 Owners
24 Strip

34

ACROSS

1 Orangeade
9 Carafe
10 Cloisters
11 Advent
12 Ascertain
13 Breton
17 Toy
19 Put up for auction
20 Pym
21 Ainley
25 Sunk fence
26 Macaws
27 Submitted
28 Nearly
29 Abrogated

DOWN

2 Relish
3 Noises
4 Estate
5 Dormitory suburb
6 Card trick
7 Mare's-tail
8 Pertinent
14 Spearmint
15 Stonechat
16 Speedwell
17 Top
18 Yam
22 Akimbo
23 Bertha
24 Accede

35

ACROSS

1 Even number
6 Reel
9 Seminaries
10 Wren
13 Revisit
15 Dramas
16 Cipher
17 Main-line station
18 Nansen
20 Single
21 Nepotic
22 Etty
25 Supervisor
26 Ewer
27 Pass friend

DOWN

1 Easy
2 Elms
3 Nantes
4 Marriage-brokers
5 Emetic
7 Earthlings
8 Lone ranger
11 Adam and Eve
12 Marionette
13 Railmen
14 Titanic
19 Nebula
20 Silver
23 Isle
24 Arid

36

ACROSS

1 Price rise
8 Specified dose
11 Eats
12 Genie
13 Acre
16 Dahlias
17 Hawking
18 Townies
20 Painter
21 Nuns
22 Smear
23 Diva
26 Secret society
27 Bassinets

DOWN

2 Race
3 Coffers
4 Rhenish
5 Side
6 Spot the winner
7 Psychiatrists
9 Headstone
10 Beggar-man
14 Livid
15 Twain
19 Semites
20 Platoon
24 Ursa
25 List

37

ACROSS

1 Timpanist
8 Roulette wheel
11 Read
12 Realm
13 Stye
16 Megaton
17 Solvent
18 Amongst
20 Gumboil
21 Offa
22 Merry
23 Swan
26 Scene-shifters
27 Stanchion

DOWN

2 Isle
3 Pattern
4 Needles
5 Soho
6 Foreign Office
7 Centre forward
9 Drum-major
10 Pestilent
14 Stage
15 Plume
19 Treason
20 Garnish
24 Knot
25 Otto

38

ACROSS

1 Triangle
5 Abroad
9 Lipstick
10 Talent
12 Pack-drill
13 Knave
14 Bang
16 Sea-lane
19 Chancel
21 Sole
24 Lydia
25 Directory
27 Enrage
28 Volition
29 Yodels
30 Sea-fight

DOWN

1 Tulips
2 Impact
3 Noted
4 Lacking
6 Blackball
7 Opera-hat
8 Dithered
11 Alps
15 Archangel
17 Scullery
18 Wandered
20 Ludo
21 Scrooge
22 Lowing
23 Cygnet
26 Cliff

39

ACROSS

6 West Yorkshire
8 Floats
9 Murdered
10 Imp
11 Owning
12 Enswathe
14 Frigate
16 Condone
20 Sergeant
23 Elapse
24 Oer
25 Doorstep
26 Trepan
27 Tenant-farmers

DOWN

1 Escaping
2 Eyesight
3 Trumpet
4 Osiris
5 Cinema
6 Well-worked-out
7 Elephant's-ears
13 Wan
15 Ace
17 Overture
18 Diameter
19 Stop off
21 Gerund
22 Attend

40

41

42

ACROSS

1 Chesterfield
8 Theorem
9 Fag-ends
11 Trefoil
12 Tessera
13 Outré
14 Panhandle
16 Windswept
19 Tench
21 Gobelin
23 Punster
24 Nullify
25 Precise
26 Orchestrator

DOWN

1 Clement
2 Ear-lobe
3 Time-lapse
4 Refit
5 Ingesta
6 Linseed
7 Station-wagon
10 Snake-charmer
15 Note-paper
17 Nobbler
18 Selfish
19 Tangent
20 Nattier
22 Noyes

ACROSS

1 Coalfields
6 Disc
10 Rogue
11 Cartwheel
12 Left-hand
13 Nylon
15 Boredom
17 Deep-sea
19 Omnibus
21 Cadence
22 Unpen
24 Ill-treat
27 Institute
28 Guise
29 Near
30 Pestilence

DOWN

1 Cork
2 Angle-iron
3 Fleet
4 Exclaim
5 Derided
7 Ideal
8 Colonnades
9 Swanherd
14 Absolution
16 Debonair
18 Sensation
20 Seizure
21 Collect
23 Pasta
25 Regal
26 Fete

ACROSS

1 Water-pistol
10 Lotus
11 Eyestrain
12 Cornfield
13 Adieu
14 Argyle
16 Reverend
18 Particle
20 Bestow
23 Roads
24 Barcelona
26 Orderlies
27 Awful
28 Francophile

DOWN

2 Alter
3 Easeful
4 Peeler
5 Steadies
6 Outrage
7 Glacial period
8 Manifest
9 Unputdownable
15 Garlands
17 Plebeian
19 Insurer
21 Eyewash
22 Presto
25 Offal

ACROSS

1 Philatelist
9 Hoodlum
10 Anthem
12 Plaudit
13 Theatre
14 Irony
15 Brasserie
17 Tawdriest
20 Clout
22 Ringlet
24 Melodic
25 Pliant
26 Terrace
27 Pret-a-porter

DOWN

2 Holiday
3 Limitable
4 Toast
5 Letters
6 Sweater
7 Shoplifters
8 Potato
11 Receptacles
16 Altimeter
18 Wangler
19 Reliant
20 Calorie
21 Ordeal
23 Tot up

ACROSS

1 Apprenticeship
10 Opposable
11 Pence
12 Intense
13 Pierce
15 Rock
17 Mock orange
18 House party
20 Seam
22 Nether
23 Bourbon
26 Heart
27 Crackdown
28 Undergraduates

DOWN

2 Pipit
3 Rising
4 Noblewoman
5 Ives
6 Emptier
7 Hindrance
8 Predetermining
9 Holier-than-thou
14 Skateboard
16 Court card
19 Erector
21 Buckra
24 Booze
25 Scar

ACROSS

1 Newcastle United
8 Rheum
9 Algicide
11 Experts
12 Resolve
13 Yodel
15 Trenchant
17 Happy hour
20 There
21 Mordent
23 Potherb
25 Autogiro
26 Norma
27 The Secret
   Garden

DOWN

1 Nursery rhyme
2 Whelp
3 Admiralty
4 Transit
5 En garde
6 Nicks
7 Tidal wave
10 Featherbrain
14 Departure
16 Catatonia
18 Outlier
19 Rapport
22 Elope
24 Eared

49

ACROSS

1 Evergreen
9 Little
10 Programme
11 Terror
12 Repentant
13 Stroke
17 Ada
19 Distant
20 Scourge
21 Esk
23 Evince
27 Relegated
28 Scathe
29 Idolising
30 Theban
31 President

DOWN

2 Verger
3 Regret
4 Rialto
5 Ermined
6 Direction
7 Starboard
8 Retriever
14 Adversity
15 Aspirates
16 Match-head
17 Ate
18 Ask
22 Slender
24 Hellas
25 Passed
26 Pennon

50

ACROSS

5 Access
8 Scourges
9 Scandal
10 Arson
11 Startling
13 Lampeter
14 Trains
17 Arc
19 Sea
20 Feline
23 Intimate
26 Palpitate
28 Nomad
29 Similar
30 Declines
31 Severn

DOWN

1 Israel
2 Noisome
3 Orangeman
4 Refuse
5 Accurate
6 Canal
7 Stagnant
12 Try
15 Rationale
16 Penalise
18 Restrain
21 Fit
22 Carmine
24 Nested
25 Eldest
27 Prise

51

ACROSS

1 Step dancing
9 Altimeter
10 Erica
11 Errand
12 Standard
13 Denote
15 Stubborn
18 Domestic
19 Egress
21 Pilchard
23 Strata
26 Sisal
27 Thrilling
28 Troublesome

DOWN

1 Seaweed
2 Eater
3 Dominates
4 Note
5 Irritate
6 Green
7 Gladden
8 Pinafore
14 Nameless
16 Bagatelle
17 Libretto
18 Deposit
20 Spangle
22 Holst
24 Amigo
25 Crib

52

ACROSS

1 Maisonette
6 Stir
10 Stake
11 Examiners
12 Mistress
13 Dwell
15 Clamant
17 Theatre
19 Inexact
21 Masonic
22 Epsom
24 Realised
27 Train-band
28 Smile
29 Lieu
30 Retrievers

DOWN

1 Mash
2 Inanimate
3 Overt
4 Element
5 Transit
7 Theme
8 Resilience
9 Windless
14 Accidental
16 Alarming
18 Tangerine
20 Terrace
21 Meander
23 Spare
25 Issue
26 Legs

53

ACROSS

1 Nemesis
5 Instant
9 Earring
10 Shebeen
11 Landgrave
12 Ditto
13 State
15 Laplander
17 Cathedral
19 Tired
22 Aitch
23 Potentate
25 Spinner
26 Barking
27 Digests
28 Elector

DOWN

1 Needles
2 Maranta
3 Sting
4 Signaller
5 Issue
6 Steadfast
7 Abetted
8 Tandoor
14 Elephants
16 Palatable
17 Classed
18 Titling
20 Realist
21 Dredger
23 Paris
24 Nerve

54

ACROSS

1 Starfish
5 Invert
9 Estonian
10 Athena
12 Emigrants
13 Prune
14 Arch
16 Support
19 Insight
21 Acre
24 Treat
25 Shelducks
27 Dismay
28 Tiresome
29 Strike
30 Lacrosse

DOWN

1 Steven
2 Antrim
3 Finer
4 Staunch
6 Notepaper
7 Executor
8 Travesty
11 Isis
15 Right back
17 Riptides
18 Assessor
20 Test
21 America
22 Across
23 Essene
26 Drear

55

ACROSS

1 Constables
9 Pomp
10 Impediment
11 Thesis
12 Curable
15 Readier
16 Eater
17 Rage
18 Snip
19 Seeds
21 Pat-ball
22 Supreme
24 Aerate
27 Particular
28 Easy
29 Recollects

DOWN

2 Ohms
3 Sierra
4 Amiable
5 Lied
6 Settler
7 Conscience
8 Apostrophe
12 Card-player
13 Right dress
14 Easel
15 Rends
19 Sleeper
20 Sundial
23 Resume
25 Eric
26 Cast

56

ACROSS

7 Steamers
9 Loader
10 Snug
11 Minute hand
12 Rancid
14 Training
15 Denied
17 Tester
20 Five-star
22 Punish
23 All the same
24 Feet
25 Linnet
26 Entirety

DOWN

1 Standard
2 Bang
3 Seemed
4 Flat race
5 Washington
6 Vernon
8 Sanity
13 Contestant
16 Entreaty
18 Respects
19 Grease
21 Inlaid
22 Presto
24 Firm

57

ACROSS

1 Rattling
5 Script
9 Suppress
10 Utopia
12 Landslide
13 Larne
14 Spar
16 Express
19 Adamant
21 Pins
24 Twist
25 Perforate
27 Contra
28 Tent-pole
29 Emends
30 Standard

DOWN

1 Rustle
2 Taping
3 Lords
4 Nastier
6 Cattle pen
7 Importer
8 Traverse
11 Sere
15 Plastered
17 Pastiche
18 Patience
20 Tope
21 Portent
22 Ladoga
23 Beheld
26 Often

ACROSS

1 Thousand
5 Ransom
9 Clashing
10 Lovers
12 Lollop
13 Lacrosse
15 Reviled
16 Fall
20 Eton
21 Disarms
25 Negation
26 Estate
28 Emetic
29 Ruminate
30 Rasher
31 Plantain

DOWN

1 Tackle
2 Orally
3 Schooner
4 Nuns
6 Aboard
7 Seedsman
8 Misdealt
11 Lateran
14 Liaison
17 Reindeer
18 Congress
19 Omission
22 Strive
23 Panama
24 Hereon
27 Bull

ACROSS

1 Chicago
5 Potters
9 Replica
10 Cantata
11 Oversight
12 Petra
13 Susie
15 Technical
17 Distemper
19 Roast
22 Chair
23 Shattered
25 Dilater
26 Ingrate
27 Riposte
28 Notelet

DOWN

1 Curious
2 Impress
3 Acids
4 Orange-tip
5 Picot
6 Tin-opener
7 Elastic
8 Sea wall
14 Execrates
16 Carnation
17 Decider
18 Snarl-up
20 Air-mail
21 Tidiest
23 Serve
24 Tight

ACROSS

1 Roughrider
9 Wary
10 Parliament
11 Regain
12 Rasping
15 Account
16 Grunt
17 Anon
18 Efts
19 Float
21 Rat-tail
22 Learner
24 Neaten
27 Eliminated
28 Ergo
29 Sonneteers

DOWN

2 Opal
3 Gallop
4 Reading
5 Dies
6 Retract
7 Ragamuffin
8 Hypnotiser
12 Road-runner
13 Short-range
14 Grill
15 Annal
19 Fitness
20 Termite
23 Rebate
25 Jinn
26 Hear

61

ACROSS

1 Public property
9 Tallies
10 Tornado
11 Left
12 Punishment
14 Aboard
15 Felonies
17 Antelope
18 Snicks
21 Ameliorate
22 Agra
24 Atlanta
25 Martini
26 Telephone kiosk

DOWN

1 Patella
2 Bolt from the blue
3 Ibid
4 Pass up
5 Obtained
6 Earth-bound
7 Travel incognito
8 Routes
13 Brilliance
16 Approach
17 Ararat
19 Seasick
20 Stamen
23 Trek

62

ACROSS

1 Glass-cutter
8 Off the point
11 Left
12 Shoo
13 Violets
15 Triumph
16 Eight
17 Rock
18 Anil
19 Hazel
21 Whopper
22 Foxtrot
23 Long
26 Stye
27 Tin Pan Alley
28 Tiddlywinks

DOWN

2 Lift
3 Situate
4 Cree
5 Two-part
6 Eons
7 All very well
8 Of no account
9 The minority
10 To the letter
14 Sitar
15 Thief
19 Helipad
20 Lorelei
24 Gigi
25 Only
26 Seek

63

ACROSS

1 Spring balance
10 In store
11 Noisome
12 Lied
13 Flare
14 Dusk
17 Hangs on
18 Exactor
19 Subzero
22 Buffalo
24 Iris
25 Spout
26 Mesh
29 Attends
30 Crouton
31 Prepared to act

DOWN

2 Postern
3 Iron
4 Gremlin
5 Aintree
6 Adit
7 Croquet
8 Field hospital
9 Neck or nothing
15 Ashes
16 Jaffa
20 Blister
21 Opposer
22 Bounced
23 Aseptic
27 Snip
28 To-do

64

ACROSS

6 Short circuits
8 Sampan
9 Interpol
10 Eon
11 Iberia
12 Execrate
14 Exalted
16 Flowing
20 Critical
23 Shiest
24 Out
25 Stirrups
26 Echoed
27 Reimbursement

DOWN

1 Corporal
2 Stone Age
3 Diviner
4 Scythe
5 Mirror
6 Soapbox orator
7 Short and sweet
13 Coo
15 Tui
17 Listener
18 Weighted
19 Closure
21 Torpid
22 Crumbs

65

ACROSS

1 Capering
9 Obituary
10 Snap
11 Exaggeration
13 Anathema
15 Dances
16 Lent
17 Brest
18 Ohms
20 School
21 Preening
23 Presbyterian
26 Oils
27 Sardines
28 Trade gap

DOWN

2 Announce
3 Expectations
4 In case
5 Gong
6 Microdot
7 Taxi
8 Gymnasts
12 Ten-pound note
14 Ate up
16 Last Post
17 Bullying
19 Mongolia
22 Enigma
24 Eire
25 Erst

66

ACROSS

1 New Year's Day
9 Char
10 White-collar
11 Icon
14 Ironing
16 Don Juan
17 Talon
18 Cads
19 Palm
20 Refer
22 Dressed
23 Relieve
24 Cuff
28 Worldly-wise
29 Once
30 Teacher's pet

DOWN

2 Echo
3 Yeti
4 Account
5 Sole
6 Abandon
7 The Crusades
8 Wrong number
12 Witch-doctor
13 Word perfect
15 Gated
16 Dover
20 Red rose
21 Resolve
25 Alec
26 Owls
27 Isle

67

ACROSS

1 Rifle
4 Downbeat
8 Niceties
9 Combined
11 Enlarge
13 Nefarious
15 On the dotted line
18 Saddle-bag
21 Endured
22 Flip-side
24 Recorder
25 Straddle
26 Kites

DOWN

1 Rendezvous
2 Face-lift
3 Enthrone
4 Disc
5 Number
6 Even so
7 Tied
10 Off-stage
12 Entombed
14 Stevedores
16 Deadlock
17 In credit
19 Driver
20 Lashed
22 Figs
23 Erse

68

ACROSS

1 Manpower
6 Joseph
9 Gemini
10 Sentinel
11 Flesh pot
12 Tidier
13 Perfect pitch
16 Leaning tower
19 Speech
21 Ructions
23 Two to one
24 Irises
25 Sydney
26 On remand

DOWN

2 Age-old
3 Pairs
4 Whipper-in
5 Rosette
6 Janet
7 Spin-drier
8 Pretence
13 Pinkerton
14 Town crier
15 Keep away
17 Torpedo
18 Unseen
20 Hooky
22 Idiom

69

ACROSS

1 Misery
4 Gift-wrap
9 Noodle
10 Stocking
12 Ruby
13 Luger
14 Fino
17 Holly berries
20 Glass slipper
23 Urge
24 Opine
25 Pegs
28 Teenager
29 Parson
30 Midnight
31 Chains

DOWN

1 Monarchy
2 Snowball
3 Rule
5 In the present
6 Tuck
7 Raisin
8 Pigeon
11 Queen's speech
15 Cycle
16 Sepia
18 Après-ski
19 Presents
21 Custom
22 Agreed
26 Magi
27 Bash

ACROSS

1 Parcel
4 Offering
9 Raisin
10 Carillon
12 Soda
13 Packs
14 Ante
17 The First Noel
20 Congregation
23 Ibis
24 Frost
25 Thaw
28 Tinselly
29 Favour
30 Pertness
31 Rave up

DOWN

1 Parasite
2 Reindeer
3 Emir
5 Frankincense
6 Epic
7 Island
8 Gander
11 Sausage rolls
15 Simon
16 Medal
18 Wishbone
19 Snowdrop
21 Tip-top
22 Dinner
26 Leon
27 Gaga

ACROSS

1 Noodles
5 Erasure
9 Aspic
10 Open-ended
11 Break of day
12 Prow
14 Desalination
18 The bee's knees
21 Pier
22 Conjecture
25 All tied up
26 Ratio
27 Enrobed
28 Nest egg

DOWN

1 Nearby
2 Osprey
3 Lock-keeper
4 Spoof
5 Elevation
6 Abed
7 Underpin
8 Endowing
13 Camel-corps
15 Absconded
16 Stoppage
17 Reveller
19 Rustle
20 Belong
23 Japan
24 Limb

ACROSS

1 Offend
4 Schubert
9 Unroll
10 Knock off
12 Ever
13 Alien
14 Peri
17 Cup and saucer
20 Resignations
23 Apse
24 Steer
25 Mete
28 Protrude
29 Malawi
30 Gateways
31 Streak

DOWN

1 Opulence
2 For keeps
3 Nile
5 Consequences
6 Unco
7 Eloped
8 Tiffin
11 All Saints Day
15 Inner
16 Berth
18 Tolerate
19 Asterisk
21 Hatpeg
22 Escort
26 Brow
27 Part